PERFECT DAY MICHIGAN

Day Trips, Weekend Getaways, and Other Escapes

Amy S. Eckert

Reedy Press
PO Box 5131
St. Louis, MO 63139
www.reedypress.com

Library of Congress Control Number: 2023938880
ISBN: 9781681064864

Printed in the United States of America
23 24 25 26 26   5 4 3 2 1

Title page images *(left to right)*:
1. Whitcomb Conservatory on Detroit's Belle Isle, courtesy of Charles Falsetti
2. Autumn Hike in Michigan, courtesy of @michiganaddicts
3. Father Marquette Statue, Mackinac Island, courtesy of Amy S. Eckert
4. La Grande Vitesse, Downtown Grand Rapids, courtesy of Experience Grand Rapids
5. Muskegon Lighthouse Winter, courtesy of Amy S. Eckert
6. Frozen Waterfall in Munising, courtesy of @naturally_hippie_chick
7. Porcupine Mountain Trail, courtesy of Amy S. Eckert
8. Holland Big Red Winter, courtesy of Amy S. Eckert

Dedication

To Bruce, who has always been my biggest supporter.

Kal-Haven Trail between Kalamazoo and South Haven
(Courtesy of South Haven Van Buren County CVB)

PERFECT DAY
MICHIGAN

Day Trips, Weekend Getaways, and Other Escapes

REEDY PRESS

Detroit city skyline
(Courtesy Amy S. Eckert)

Contents

Images courtesy of Amy S. Eckert

CANADA STEAMSHIP LINES

Upper Tahquamenon Falls (Courtesy of Amy S. Eckert)

Introduction

Michigan is a large and incredibly diverse state. Its borders are defined by four of the five Great Lakes, forming a nearly 3,300-mile shoreline, second among US states only to Alaska. No other American state claims more lighthouses than Michigan does (129), and the state's 97,000 square miles of land include tens of thousands of islands, lakes, and waterfalls. Its four distinct seasons make Michigan a great destination for year-round fun, including skiing and surfing, brilliant fall leaf-peeping tours and award-winning wine tastings, long-distance hiking, and sailing. And in addition to offering spectacular outdoor recreation, Michigan is home to some of the most vibrant and creative urban centers in the country.

It would take a lifetime to explore all that Michigan has to offer. But what if you had only one day? That's the premise behind *Perfect Day Michigan*. Here in these pages, I've listed itineraries to help you make the most of your limited time in Michigan, my home state. Here it is that I have spent my life hiking, museum hopping, snowshoeing, and beachcombing before sitting down to write all about it.

Welcome to Michigan. I hope you have a perfect day!

SUPERIOR
COPPER HARBOR
KEWEENAW PENINSULA
HANCOCK
26
ONTONAGON
PORCUPINE MOUNTAINS WILDERNESS STATE PARK
L'ANSE
GRAND ISLAND
45
BRUCE CROSSING
28
BESSEMER
LAKE GOGEBIC
OTTOWA NATIONAL FOREST
41
MARQUETTE
MUNISING
MICHIGAN
SENEY NWR
WATERSMEET
141
2
TRENARY
41
HIAWATHA NATIONAL FOREST
MANISTIQ
2
NORWAY
2
ESCANABA
41
35
MANITOU ISLANDS
PORCUPINE MOUNTAINS WILDERNESS STATE PARK
28
BESSEMER
31
LUDINGTON
SILVER LAKE SAND DUNES
31
MADISON
MILWAUKEE
LAKE

PORCUPINE MOUNTAINS WILDERNESS STATE PARK

MICHIGAN'S LARGEST state park lies in the western corner of Michigan's Upper Peninsula. With its northern border on the Lake Superior shore, its remaining 60,000 acres are a paradise of old-growth forest and rushing waterfalls, crystal-clear lakes, and craggy basalt mountains. The Porkies, as they are commonly known, are famous for the mirror-smooth **Lake of the Clouds** and the beautiful, rocky scenery alongside the **Presque Isle River**, the park's largest. But there are countless similarly spectacular natural features in this slice of God's Country—Mirror Lake, Lost Lake, and Trap Falls among them—and you can explore them all along 90 miles of hiking trails.

The Porcupine Mountains are most easily explored in the warm-weather months, from mid-May to mid-October. The park's superb visitors center is also open over those months and worth visiting for its excellent displays that detail the local flora and fauna as well as the region's copper mining and lumbering history. But the mountains are lovely in winter, too. Explore the trails via snowshoes or skis and check out the lantern-lit trail on the Lake Superior Loop.

Lake of the Clouds

Hwy. 107 • 906-885-5275 • michigandnr.com/parksandtrails

The shining jewel of the Porcupine Mountains is the Lake of the Clouds. Set atop a basalt escarpment, on bright days the water's glassy surface reflects the clouds overhead, allowing the high-elevation lake to lay double claim to its name. It's easy enough to view the Lake of the Clouds from a scenic overlook accessed via car from Highway 107. But if you have the time and energy, it's worth hiking along the **Escarpment Trail**, where you'll enjoy unmatched views of one of Michigan's prettiest inland lakes and the Porcupine Mountains' most photographed natural attraction. If you're really inclined to linger, reserve a backcountry campsite or an overnight at a rustic cabin, all of which lie along the banks of Lake of the Clouds. Visit the park's website for details, and reserve well in advance at these exceptionally popular sites.

Lake of the Clouds (Courtesy of Amy S. Eckert)

Manabezho Falls, Presque Isle River (Courtesy of Amy S. Eckert)

Presque Isle East and West River Trails

Hwy. 519 • 906-885-5275 • michigandnr.com/parksandtrails

☑ Fragrant hemlock trees shelter the East and West River Trails and frame views of one of Michigan's loveliest river corridors. Accessed by a parking lot off Highway 519 just north of South Boundary Road, the trail skirts the edge of a rocky canyon that looks down over the Presque Isle River. A series of cascades—the **Nawadaha, Manido, and Manabezho Falls**—makes the already pretty river corridor especially beautiful. Sprays of delicate wildflowers and trees adorned with jewel-tone lichen and shelf fungus brighten the trail. Along the way, the path passes over tortured tree roots and carpets of moss, climbs rocky staircases, links to the **North Country National Scenic Trail**, and crosses over the river via a bridge that joins the East and West River Trails into a 2.5-mile loop. The Presque Isle River empties into Lake Superior. It's an easy walk from the trail to the beach and the Presque Isle Rustic Campground.

Syl's Cafe

713 River St., Ontonagon • 906-884-2522 • facebook.com/sylscafeonto

☑ Located in the heart of Ontonagon, the entryway to the Porcupine Mountains Wilderness State Park, and set on the banks of the Ontonagon River, Syl's Cafe is a local favorite and an inexpensive place to fill up before or after an active day in the park. Syl's bakery case is filled in the mornings with fresh-baked donuts, flaky fruit strudels, and cookies. Simple, homemade comfort food is the rule on the take-out and dine-in menus. At breakfast, fill up on hearty omelets and skillets before heading out on your hike. Homemade soups, grilled cheese, and BLT sandwiches make up the lunchtime fare, with pot roast, pizza, and burgers served at dinnertime.

But the real treat at Syl's Cafe is its pasties, the Cornish-inspired hot meat and vegetable pies famous in the Upper Peninsula as the traditional lunchtime staple for miners. You can dine outside in warm-weather months at one of the sidewalk umbrella tables.

Freshly baked pasty
(Courtesy of @darrenmakesfood)

Nearby Alternatives

Outdoors: Escarpment Trail

Considered one of the most scenic hiking trails in Michigan, the 8.5-mile, out-and-back Escarpment Trail climbs quickly upward from the parking lot before following the top of the escarpment from which it takes its name. The trail provides unsurpassed views of the Porcupine Mountains and Lake of the Clouds.

Hwy. 107
906-885-5275
michigandnr.com/parksandtrails

Activity: Lake Gogebic State Park

Paddling, swimming, and fishing are popular pastimes at Lake Gogebic, the largest inland lake in the western UP. Lake Gogebic State Park sits on the lake's southwest corner, some 35 miles south of Porcupine Mountains State Park. Nearly one mile of lake frontage lies within the park, which includes 30 campsites.

N 9995 Hwy. M-64, Marinesco
906-842-3341
michigandnr.com/parksandtrails

Outdoors: Porcupine Mountains Ski Area

The Porcupine Mountains claim one of the most beautiful natural ski areas in all of Michigan, with views of icy Lake Superior to the north and the Porkies covered in 200 inches of snow all around. The mountain features groomed trails, a terrain park, and backcountry skiing cut through the glades.

Hwy. 107
906-885-5209
michigan.gov/skitheporkies

Tour: Old Victoria

In the late 1800s, copper mining boomed in the Porcupine Mountains, and the historically reconstructed residences at Old Victoria recall the lives of the people who worked those mines. Visitors can tour the homes at the site, affiliated with the **National Park Service**, during warm-weather months.

25401 Victoria Dam Rd.
906-886-2617
nps.gov/places/old-victoria.htm

Trip Planning

Porcupine Mountains Wilderness State Park

33303 Headquarters Rd., Ontonagon
906-885-5275
michigandnr.com/parksandtrails

LAKE SUPERIOR
KEWEENAW PENINSULA
HANCOCK
ONTONAGON
PORCUPINE MOUNTAINS WILDERNESS STATE PARK
L'ANSE
BESSEMER
LAKE GOGEBIC
OTTOWA NATIONAL FOREST
BRUCE CROSSING
WATERSMEET
MICHIGAN
MARQUETTE
GRAND ISLAND
MUNISING
SENEY NWR
HIAWATHA NATIONAL FOREST
MANISTIQUE
MANITOU ISLANDS
LUDINGTON
SILVER LAKE SAND DUNES
SHELBY
COPPER HARBOR
KEWEENAW PENINSULA

COPPER HARBOR

COPPER HARBOR SITS at the northernmost tip of the Keweenaw Peninsula, an 80-mile-long finger of the Upper Peninsula that juts out into Lake Superior. The peninsula's rich copper mining history lies at the heart of this northerly part of Michigan, as the town's name suggests. You'll find ample opportunity to explore this heritage at mining museums and on tours of abandoned mine shafts, many of which are protected and managed as part of the **Keweenaw National Historical Park**. You'll also find lots of gift and rock shops throughout the Keweenaw Peninsula that sell raw copper and polished copper jewelry.

As interesting as the Copper Harbor area's mining history is, the area's spectacular natural beauty and opportunities for outdoor recreation rank as the chief draws for travelers. Forest-covered basalt mountains offer many scenic overlooks and challenging hiking and mountain biking trails. Inland lakes, like Lake Fanny Hooe, Lac La Belle, and Portage Lake, offer opportunities for boating or trout and bass fishing. And mighty Lake Superior, with her powerful surf, agate-strewn beaches, and stately lighthouses, is a constant draw.

Fort Wilkins Historic State Park

15223 US-41 • 906-289-4215
michigandnr.com/parksandtrails

☑ The restored fort that sits just outside Copper Harbor was constructed in 1844, when the federal government deemed it wise to establish military protection of the region's copper shipping routes. Visitors to Fort Wilkins can learn about midcentury military life walking through the re-created officers' quarters, barracks, supply buildings, and the remainder of the fort. A living history program with interpretive actors adds life and context to Fort Wilkins.

Outside of the state park's historical features, Fort Wilkins provides access to pristine natural beauty and outdoor recreation. The park features a modern campground on the shores of **Lake Fanny Hooe**, popular for its swimming beach, boating, and fishing. There's also frontage on Lake Manganese and Lake Superior as well as two 1860s lighthouses, biking, hiking, and mountain biking trails. In winter, the trails transform into beautiful areas for snowshoeing and cross-country skiing.

Fort Wilkins Historic State Park
(Courtesy of Visit Keweenaw)

Keweenaw National Historical Park (Courtesy of Visit Keweenaw)

Keweenaw National Historical Park

25970 Red Jacket Rd., Calumet
906-337-3168 • nps.gov/kewe

✔ In 1843, half a dozen years before prospectors flooded into California, copper miners headed to northern Michigan and the Keweenaw Peninsula in the nation's first mining rush. Thousands of miners, entrepreneurs, and their families worked in more than 100 mines in the area until the industry went bust in the early 1900s.

The Keweenaw National Historical Park follows the history of copper on the peninsula from its earliest mining operations some 7,000 years ago. Among the sites worth visiting are the Copper Range Historical Museum, with artifacts related to those living and working in the mines; the Coppertown Mining Museum, which focuses on underground operations; and the Delaware Copper Mine, where visitors can take a self-guided mine tour. The most popular of the historical sites is always the **Quincy Mine**, which includes a guided cog-rail tram ride into what was once one of the world's largest copper mines.

Keweenaw Mountain Lodge

14252 US-41 • 906-289-4403 • keweenawmountainlodge.com

✓ The Keweenaw Mountain Lodge traces its history to the early 1930s, when, at the peak of the Great Depression and with local copper mines shuttered, a large team of unemployed locals was commissioned by the Works Progress Administration (WPA) to construct this golf course and resort grounds. Among the most remarkable structures built on the site of the Keweenaw Mountain Lodge is its impressively large dining room. The fieldstone fireplace and the massive beams of the log cabin–style building were taken from the surrounding property.

Dinner menus include house-made pasta, lamb ragu, pork tenderloin, and vegetable curries, and are limited in scope to allow kitchen staff time for hands-on food preparation. The head chef, Widad Mueller, was born in Lebanon and has lived around the world. Her international experiences show up on the menu in the way of a fresh hummus appetizer, kebab patties, and Chinese dumplings.

Keweenaw Mountain Lodge (Courtesy of Visit Keweenaw)

Nearby Alternatives

Discover: Brockway Mountain

Crest Brockway Mountain via Brockway Mountain Drive, which snakes its way upward to reveal 360-degree views of the mountains and Lake Superior. Numerous parking areas make it easy to linger over the view, which you will want to do, particularly at the peak of fall color and at sunset.

Brockway Mountain Dr.
visitkeweenaw.com

Outdoors: Isle Royale National Park

Copper Harbor is the gateway to Isle Royale National Park, set in Lake Superior. The island is known for its untamed North Country wilderness: craggy sandstone cliff faces, thick evergreen and beech forests, scenic hiking trails, fishing, and paddling. Ferries make the 3.5-hour journey to the island from mid-April through October.

Isle Royale
906-482-0984
nps.gov/isro

Discover: Quincy Mine

A two-hour tour of the Quincy Mine, known as "Old Reliable," sheds light on the workings of one of the earliest copper mines in northern Michigan, and one of its most productive. After exploring the mine's massive hoist house, visitors descend into the mine by way of a cog-rail tram.

49750 US-41, Hancock
906-482-3101
quincymine.com

Museum: A.E. Seaman Mineral Museum

This outstanding museum displays a fantastic array of rocks and minerals from around the world: vivid blue azurite, sparkling calcite, bright yellow sulfur, and one of the country's finest fluorescent mineral exhibits, brilliantly illuminated in black light. Check out the Copper Pavilion, with a 19-ton copper mass from Lake Superior.

1404 E Sharon Ave., Houghton
906-487-2572
museum.mtu.edu

Trip Planning

Visit Keweenaw

56638 Calumet Ave., Calumet
906-337-4579
visitkeweenaw.com

LAKE SUPERIOR
COPPER HARBOR
KEWEENAW PENINSULA
HANCOCK
ONTONAGON
PORCUPINE MOUNTAINS WILDERNESS STATE PARK
L'ANSE
BESSEMER
LAKE GOGEBIC
BRUCE CROSSING
OTTOWA NATIONAL FOREST
WATERSMEET
MICHIGAN
GRAND ISLAND
MUNISING
SENEY NWR
TRENARY
HIAWATHA NATIONAL FOREST
MANISTIQUE
NORWAY
ESCANABA
WISCONSIN
MENOMINEE
MANITOU ISLANDS
LUDINGTON
SILVER LAKE SAND DUNES
SHELBY
MADISON
MILWAUKEE
LAKE
MARQUETTE
HIGAN

MARQUETTE

THE UPPER PENINSULA'S largest city sits on the shores of Lake Superior, the whole city clustered along the waterfront as if to collectively admire the views of the Great Lake. The vista includes the harbor's imposing Ore Dock, once used to load ships with tons of iron ore taken from upper Great Lakes mines. But the scene also includes views of colorful boats, the brilliant red Marquette Harbor Lighthouse, and the relentless Lake Superior surf washing over rocky islets and sandy South Beach.

Outdoor recreation is a key attraction to those who live in and visit Marquette. The **Iron Ore Heritage Trail**, a 47-mile multiuse path, is popular with hikers, cyclists, and mountain bikers. The **Noquemanon Trail Network** manages more than 150 miles of hiking, biking, and ski trails in the Central UP as well as the 120-mile Hiawatha Water Trail. Campgrounds and state parks lie scattered around Marquette, and you can access the **North Country National Scenic Trail** from here, too. Snow doesn't stop the outdoor action. Marquette receives an average of 155 inches of snow each year, making this a great spot for skiers, snowshoers, and snowmobilers.

Marquette Bay

Lakeshore Blvd. • 906-228-7749 • travelmarquette.com

✓ Lake Superior dominates life in Marquette. In summer, head to **McCarty's Cove**, where the sandy beach and a lifeguard (from Memorial Day through Labor Day) make this a popular family getaway. A paved walkway, which piggybacks on the **Iron Ore Heritage Trail** for several miles, skirts the edge of Marquette Bay. Hop aboard a bike, lace up your running shoes, or pull out the kids' stroller and enjoy the area's great natural beauty, just a short walk from downtown Marquette.

Downtown Marquette features plenty of family-friendly restaurants that exploit their views of Marquette Bay, many of them offering outdoor seating. Consider **Sol Azteca**, serving Mexican food; the **Vierling Restaurant** and **Marquette Harbor Brewery**; and **Provisions MQT** café. Afterward, drive to the Mt. Marquette Overlook, which rises 1,200 feet in elevation, a perennially popular lookout over the entire Marquette Bay, including city views, Lake Superior, and the surrounding Huron Mountains.

Marquette Bay
(Courtesy of Aaron Peterson)

Marquette Harbor Lighthouse (Courtesy of Amy S. Eckert)

Marquette Harbor Lighthouse

300 N Lakeshore Blvd. • 906-226-2006
facebook.com/mqtmaritime.museum

☑ In a region packed with lighthouses, the Marquette Harbor Lighthouse ranks among one of the loveliest. The brilliant red lighthouse stands high above the water, set upon a rocky peninsula that juts out into Lake Superior. The lighthouse is one of the oldest structures in Marquette, originally built in 1853 and renovated or expanded in 1866 and again in 1909. Visitors can walk the grounds of the lighthouse year-round but do watch for slippery conditions in the winter.

Guided tours of the lighthouse may be organized at the adjacent **Marquette Maritime Museum**, which is worth visiting in its own right. The small museum is jam-packed with displays about Lake Superior shipwrecks (including the *Edmund Fitzgerald*), early lifesaving and Coast Guard operations, a 3-D breeches buoy exhibition, and one of the Great Lakes' largest collections of Fresnel lenses.

Steinhaus

102 W Washington St., #115 • 906-273-1531 • steinhausmqt.com

Classic German dishes make up the lion's share of the menu at this popular downtown Marquette restaurant, located just one block from the beautiful Lake Superior shore. Each morning, the kitchen staff gets to work shaping dozens of homemade soft pretzels, stuffing house-made sausage casings, and adding the savory fillings to fresh pierogies. Brunch revolves around locally raised eggs and pan-fried speck. Entrées include classic Jägerschnitzel, vegetarian spätzle, and Wiener schnitzel, but the dishes change depending upon what's currently in season. You'll also see creative craft cocktail specials, beer, and wine.

If Steinhaus's commitment to creating quality German-inspired dishes is sincere, so is its commitment to sourcing local, ethically produced ingredients. Local farms supply the restaurant's free-range eggs; pastured pork, beef, and chicken; organic herbs and vegetables; and raw honey.

House-made pretzels at Steinhaus
(Courtesy of Steinhaus)

Nearby Alternatives

Museum: Marquette Regional History Center

Learn how Marquette developed into the city it is today at this excellent history museum. The museum's oldest artifacts relate to the Ojibwa people, who first made their mark on this landscape 11,000 years ago. Other exhibits relate to local copper culture, the region's native flora and fauna, and local Yooper inventions and innovations.

145 W Spring St.
906-226-3571
marquettehistory.org

Outdoors: Iron Ore Heritage Trail

Outdoor enthusiasts who utilize the 47-mile Iron Ore Heritage Trail, which travels through downtown Marquette, can simultaneously learn about the region's 160-year mining history. Interpretive signs explain Native American and mining heritage and point out important highlights like abandoned open-pit mines. The trail is popular with hikers, runners, and cyclists, and, in winter, with snowshoers and cross-country skiers.

Marquette Bay
ironoreheritage.com

Outdoors: Presque Isle Park

Occupying a 323-acre forested peninsula north of Marquette, Presque Isle Park is one of the area's most popular destinations for outdoorsy types. Besides the outstanding vistas of Lake Superior, visitors can bike the peninsula's perimeter, hike the trails through its central forest, or visit **Blackrocks**, where in summer locals dive into the surf from atop 15-foot cliffs.

N Lakeshore Blvd. at Island Beach Rd.
906-228-0435
marquettemi.gov

Outdoors: Noquemanon Trail Network

More than 150 miles of trails throughout the central UP are managed by the NTN, which is centered around Marquette. During "dirt season," the trails draw hikers and mountain bikers. When the snow flies, Nordic skiers and fat-tire bikers arrive. Check the network's website to determine which trails are open to which activities.

906-235-6861
noquetrails.org

Trip Planning

Travel Marquette

117 W Washington St.
906-228-7749
travelmarquette.com

LAKE SUPERIOR
COPPER HARBOR
KEWEENAW PENINSULA
HANCOCK
ONTONAGON
PORCUPINE MOUNTAINS WILDERNESS STATE PARK
L'ANSE
BESSEMER
LAKE GOGEBIC
OTTOWA NATIONAL FOREST
BRUCE CROSSING
WATERSMEET
MARQUETTE
GRAND ISLAND
MUNISING
MICHIGAN
SENEY NWR
TRENARY
HIAWATHA NATIONAL FOREST
MANISTIQUE
NORWAY
ESCANABA
WISCONSIN
MENOMINEE
MANITOU ISLANDS
LUDINGTON
SILVER LAKE SAND DUNES
SHELBY
MADISON
MILWAUKEE
LAKE MICHIGAN
GRAND ISLAND
MUNISING
SENEY NWR
HIAWATHA NATIONAL FOREST

MUNISING

LIFE REVOLVES AROUND Lake Superior in Munising, and in particular, around the **Pictured Rocks National Lakeshore** just east of town. The little UP community of 2,000 year-round residents explodes with the addition of more than 1.2 million visitors in the summer, when brilliant sunny days and Lake Superior's calm waters make the lakeshore's colorful cliff faces especially vibrant and easier to visit.

Because of Munising's small size and the popularity of its national park, visitors to this UP community are wise to make travel plans well in advance of their arrival, particularly if they want to camp within the Pictured Rocks boundaries. Outside of the national park, Munising offers half a dozen beautiful and easily reached waterfalls, access to the North Country National Scenic Trail, and intact shipwrecks, which can be visited on guided scuba dives or via a glass-bottom boat tour. Don't overlook Munising's appeal as a wintertime destination. Munising is a popular snowmobiling destination. The Pictured Rocks are particularly beautiful in winter, when the park's cliffside seeps form spectacular, colorful icicles. And you'll avoid the large summertime crowds.

Pictured Rocks National Lakeshore

1505 Sand Point Rd. • 906-387-3700
nps.gov/piro

✓ Splashed by the surf of Lake Superior, famous for its soaring sandstone cliffs, dense with thick hardwood and pine forest, and crisscrossed by nearly 100 miles of hiking trails, Pictured Rocks National Lakeshore ranks as one of the most popular national parks in the Great Lakes. Pictured Rocks became the nation's first national lakeshore when it received the designation in 1966. But this scenic landscape had long been appreciated by locals, who boarded the first cruises of the Pictured Rocks shoreline in the 1920s, aboard the ships of the Cleveland Cliff Iron Company.

The Pictured Rocks are most commonly visited in summer, when temperate weather and the breezes off **Lake Superior** make this region an ideal getaway for backpackers, hikers, campers, and anglers. But spring introduces a carpet of wildflowers to this national lakeshore. The brilliant foliage of hardwood trees brings a riot of fall color. And in winter, snowshoers can view the cliff faces covered with icy stalactites.

Miners Castle, Pictured Rocks National Lakeshore (Courtesy of Amy S. Eckert)

Pictured Rocks Cruises (Courtesy of Amy S. Eckert)

Pictured Rocks Cruises

100 City Park Dr. • 906-387-2379 • picturedrocks.com

✓ The imposing multicolored cliff faces of **Pictured Rocks National Lakeshore** stretch 15 miles in length, their golden- and russet-hued surfaces sculpted by Lake Superior into spectacular caves, arches, and towering stone pillars. And while it's possible to see some of these outcroppings via hiking trails and overlooks, the easiest way to view the rock formations is from the water.

Pictured Rocks Cruises escorts visitors to the most beautiful of these cliff faces, including the most famous formation, **Miners Castle**. Cruises depart from the waterfront in downtown Munising, and include commentary related to the history and lore of this national park. Daytime cruises provide a fun way to cool off on a hot summer day; evening cruises reveal the cliffs in the red and orange glow of the setting sun. Visitors interested in a more challenging Pictured Rocks experience can book one of the cruise company's guided kayaking trips to the lakeshore.

Tracey's

815 W Munising Ave. • 906-387-8000
roam-inn.com/traceys

✓ Set overlooking Lake Superior and within the **Roam Inn** (a great place to spend the night), Tracey's offers the finest food in Munising, and the restaurant serves it up in a casual, relaxed atmosphere. The inn and its restaurant occupy what was once a lakeside residence, with the restaurant and its large outdoor dining area facing South Bay. The restaurant's interior and large bar area are furnished in blond wood and pale gray hues, giving the space a light, airy look, and artwork throughout the building highlights images of **Pictured Rocks National Lakeshore**.

Entrée selections at Tracey's vary by the season, but often include Lake Superior whitefish and meat dishes prepared with locally sourced cheeses and veggies. The menu also includes a nice array of sushi and ramen dishes. Michigan beers and ciders are well represented on the drinks list, and house cocktails include Michigan fruit and spirits.

Tracey's (Courtesy of UPTravel)

Nearby Alternatives

Discover: Munising Falls

In a region known for waterfalls, Munising Falls rank among the most easily accessible. A paved walkway leads to the falls from the **Pictured Rocks Munising Falls Visitor Center**. The 800-foot trail leads through a shaded canyon and alongside Munising Creek to the falls, which drop 50 feet over a beautiful sandstone cliff face.

1505 Sand Point Rd.
906-387-3700
nps.gov/piro

Outdoors: Grand Island National Recreation Area

Grand Island sits surrounded by Lake Superior, about a half mile offshore from Munising. The island is popular with day-trippers who visit to bike, hike, paddle, and fish, but there are multiple campsites, some easily accessed by kayakers. Grand Island is part of the **Hiawatha National Forest** and accessed by ferry service from Munising.

Grand Island Rd.
906-428-5800
fs.usda.gov

Restaurant: Muldoon's Pasties

If there's any food synonymous with the UP, it's pasties, and Muldoon's pasties are among the best. Introduced by Cornish miners in the mid-1800s, the flaky pies are traditionally filled with a hearty mix of diced beef, potatoes, onions, carrots, and rutabaga. Enjoy them hot, with or without gravy, or buy them frozen to enjoy later.

1246 M-28 W.
906-387-5880
muldoonspasties.com

Discover: Grand Marais

This tiny town forms the eastern gateway to the Pictured Rocks, a quieter option to Munising (although farther from the park's main attractions). Go rock hunting at **Agate Beach**. Hike to the Sable Falls, one mile out of Grand Marais. And tour **Au Sable Light Station**, just inside the border of **Pictured Rocks National Lakeshore**.

906-494-2447
grandmaraismichigan.com

Trip Planning

Munising Visitors Bureau

129 E Munising Ave.
906-387-1717
munising.org

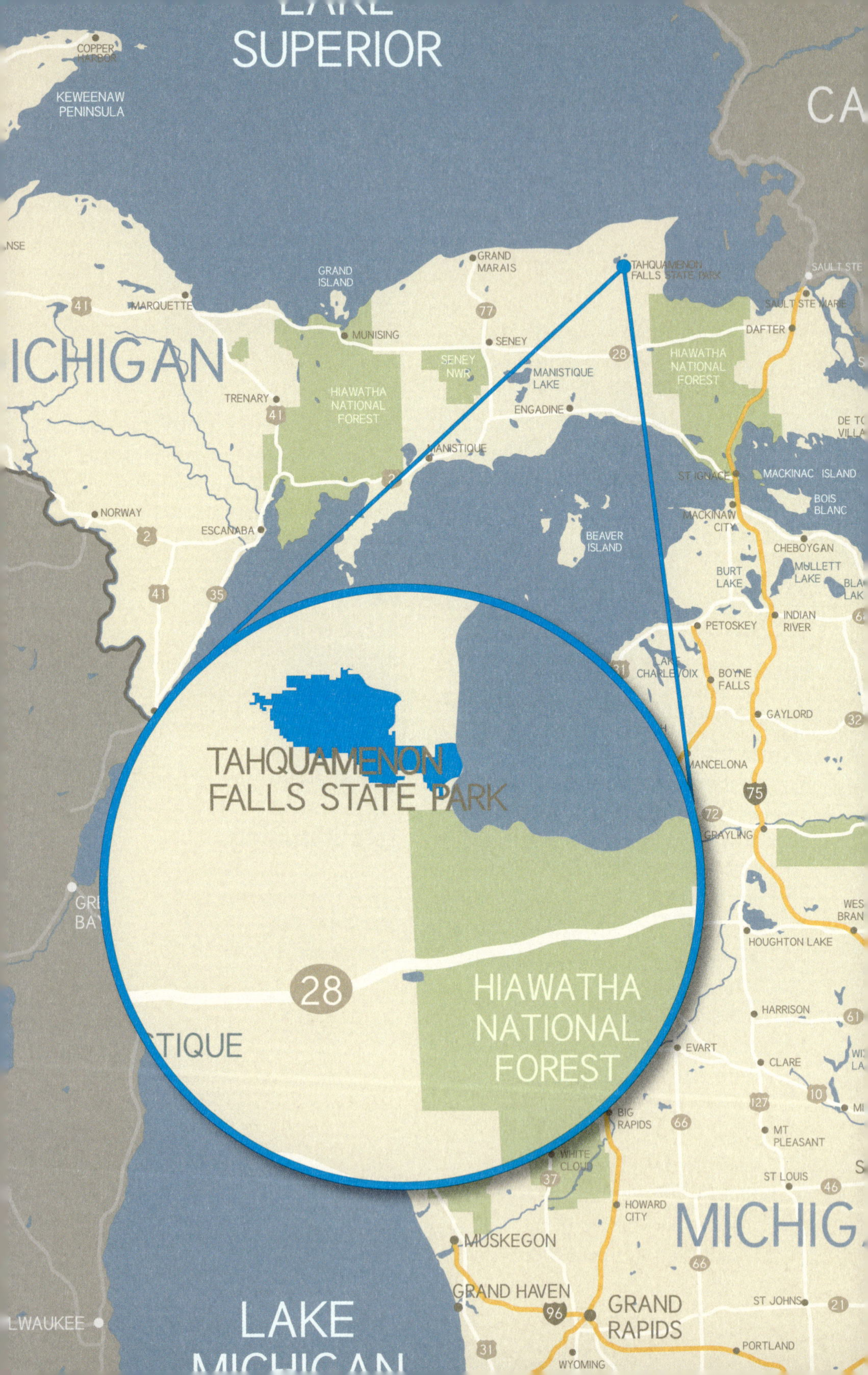
LAKE SUPERIOR
COPPER HARBOR
KEWEENAW PENINSULA
GRAND ISLAND
GRAND MARAIS
TAHQUAMENON FALLS STATE PARK
SAULT STE MARIE
MARQUETTE
MICHIGAN
MUNISING
SENEY
DAFTER
SENEY NWR
MANISTIQUE LAKE
HIAWATHA NATIONAL FOREST
TRENARY
ENGADINE
MANISTIQUE
ST IGNACE
MACKINAC ISLAND
BOIS BLANC
MACKINAW CITY
NORWAY
ESCANABA
BEAVER ISLAND
CHEBOYGAN
BURT LAKE
MULLETT LAKE
INDIAN RIVER
PETOSKEY
LAKE CHARLEVOIX
BOYNE FALLS
GAYLORD
MANCELONA
GRAYLING
HOUGHTON LAKE
HARRISON
EVART
CLARE
BIG RAPIDS
MT PLEASANT
WHITE CLOUD
ST LOUIS
HOWARD CITY
MUSKEGON
GRAND HAVEN
GRAND RAPIDS
ST JOHNS
PORTLAND
WYOMING
LAKE MICHIGAN
TAHQUAMENON FALLS STATE PARK
28
HIAWATHA NATIONAL FOREST

TAHQUAMENON FALLS STATE PARK

THIS BELOVED STATE park encompasses nearly 50,000 acres in the northeastern corner of Michigan's Upper Peninsula. At first blush, you wouldn't think this park should be so popular since only a tiny portion of the park borders Lake Superior. Instead, most of the park's real estate borders the Tahquamenon River, a serpentine waterway that passes through dense Northwoods forest roughly midway between Munising and Sault Ste. Marie.

But even Michiganders who don't consider themselves outdoorsy types make a point of visiting Tahquamenon. The appeal? The park's waterfalls. Picture-postcard perfect, beautifully flanked by towering white pine trees (Michigan's state tree), famously root-beer brown in color, and easily accessed via paved walkways, the Tahquamenon River's waterfalls make this state park one of Michigan's most popular. Access the park via a day trip from **Sault Ste. Marie** (expect a one-hour drive) or invest a full day. Hotel rooms and restaurants can be found in nearby **Paradise** or **Newberry**. Better yet, reserve a campsite within Tahquamenon Falls State Park, and immerse yourself in an unforgettable UP destination.

Upper and Lower Tahquamenon Falls

41382 W M-123, Paradise • 906-492-3415 • michigandnr.com/parksandtrails

The Upper Tahquamenon Falls rank as Michigan's biggest waterfall and one of the largest waterfalls east of the Mississippi River. The Upper Falls measure more than 200 feet in width and drop 50 feet. On its way to Lake Superior, the river passes through cedar and hemlock stands that infuse the water with brown, root-beer-colored tannins. Viewing platforms sit along a pleasant, flat walkway from the parking lot. For a closer vantage point, follow one of two long stairways to the base of the falls (each close to 100 steps).

The Lower Tahquamenon Falls are four miles downstream and comprised of five smaller cascades encircling a small island. Reach the island via rowboat or canoe—a park concession rents the popular boats in summer—or walk the hiking trails and footbridge. Once there, you'll be able to access the shallow water, where visitors love to splash and cool off on hot summer days.

Upper Tahquamenon Falls (Courtesy of Amy S. Eckert)

River Trail (Courtesy of Amy S. Eckert)

River Trail

41382 W M-123, Paradise • 906-492-3415 • michigandnr.com/parksandtrails

✔ A paved road links the Upper and Lower Tahquamenon Falls. But if you have the time and energy, opt for the River Trail, which leads four miles one way through the park's beautiful forest and along the banks of the Tahquamenon River. Over twisted tree roots and carpets of thick cypress and hemlock needles, alongside gnarled tree trunks, past colorful spring wildflowers, and over boardwalks leading across the river's wetlands, the moderately difficult River Trail rewards hikers with the quieter side of **Tahquamenon Falls State Park**. One option for exploring the trail is to begin at the Lower Falls and enjoy lunch at the **Tahquamenon Falls Brewery** near the Upper Falls before returning to your starting point.

The River Trail is equally beautiful in winter. Strap on snowshoes for a moderately challenging trek through a thick blanket of snow and admire the Tahquamenon Falls adorned with amber-colored icicles, free of summertime crowds.

Tahquamenon Falls Brewery & Pub

24019 Upper Falls Dr., Paradise • 906-492-3300 • tahquamenonfallsbrewery.com

☑ End a tiring day hiking, paddling, and playing at the Tahquamenon Falls with a meal at the Tahquamenon Falls Brewery & Pub. Designed in the style of a rustic Northwoods lodge, the pub features a large fieldstone fireplace, and its walls are decorated with taxidermied moose and the pelts of black bears and wolves. The family-friendly menu includes burgers, salads, locally caught whitefish, and that UP classic, the pasty. You'll see the brewery's fermentation tanks behind the bar. Seasonally available beers include Lumberjack Lager, Black Bear Stout, Falls Tannin, White Pine Pilsner, and Porcupine Pale Ale.

Tahquamenon Falls Brewery is furnished with a sprawling deck and shaded picnic tables, where you can indulge in an ice cream cone or a cold drink if you're not in the mood for a big meal. The facility also includes a nice gift shop selling Tahquamenon Falls and UP-themed souvenirs.

Tahquamenon Falls Brewery & Pub (Courtesy of UPTravel)

Nearby Alternatives

Museum: Great Lakes Shipwreck Museum

You could easily spend half a day at the Great Lakes Shipwreck Museum, a gem of a museum set within a historic lifesaving station and lighthouse from 1861. Museum artifacts tell the stories of ships lost in nearby **Shipwreck Alley**, including the most famous, the *Edmund Fitzgerald*. Open May through September.

18335 N Whitefish Point Rd.
888-492-3747
shipwreckmuseum.com

Discover: Whitefish Point Bird Observatory

Considered one of Michigan's finest birdwatching hot spots, the Whitefish Point Bird Observatory sits on a spit of land that juts into Lake Superior, a natural migration corridor for hundreds of birds. Bird sightings are always weather dependent, but you may spot sizable hawk and owl migrations, sandhill cranes, common loons, and endangered piping plovers.

16914 N Whitefish Point Rd.
517-580-7364
(Michigan Audubon in Okemos)
wpbo.org

Restaurant: Brown Fisheries Fish House

Fill up on fresh Lake Superior whitefish caught within hours of hitting your plate. Family-owned Brown Fisheries Fish House is locally famous for its delicious, flavorful fish, serving whitefish sandwiches and two- or three-piece meals in baskets. Opening hours always depend on the size and availability of the day's catch.

32638 W M-123
906-492-3901
facebook.com/brownfisheriesfishhouse

Museum: Tahquamenon Logging Museum

Photographs and artifacts at this small museum, open only in summer, recount the importance of Michigan's UP for the logging industry in the 19th century. Visitors can learn about the effort required to log the region and explore life in a logging camp. Lumberjack shows are held periodically throughout the season.

7964 M-123, Newberry
906-293-3700
tahquamenonloggingmuseum.org

Trip Planning

Tahquamenon Falls State Park

41382 W M-123, Paradise
906-492-3415
michigandnr.com/parksandtrails

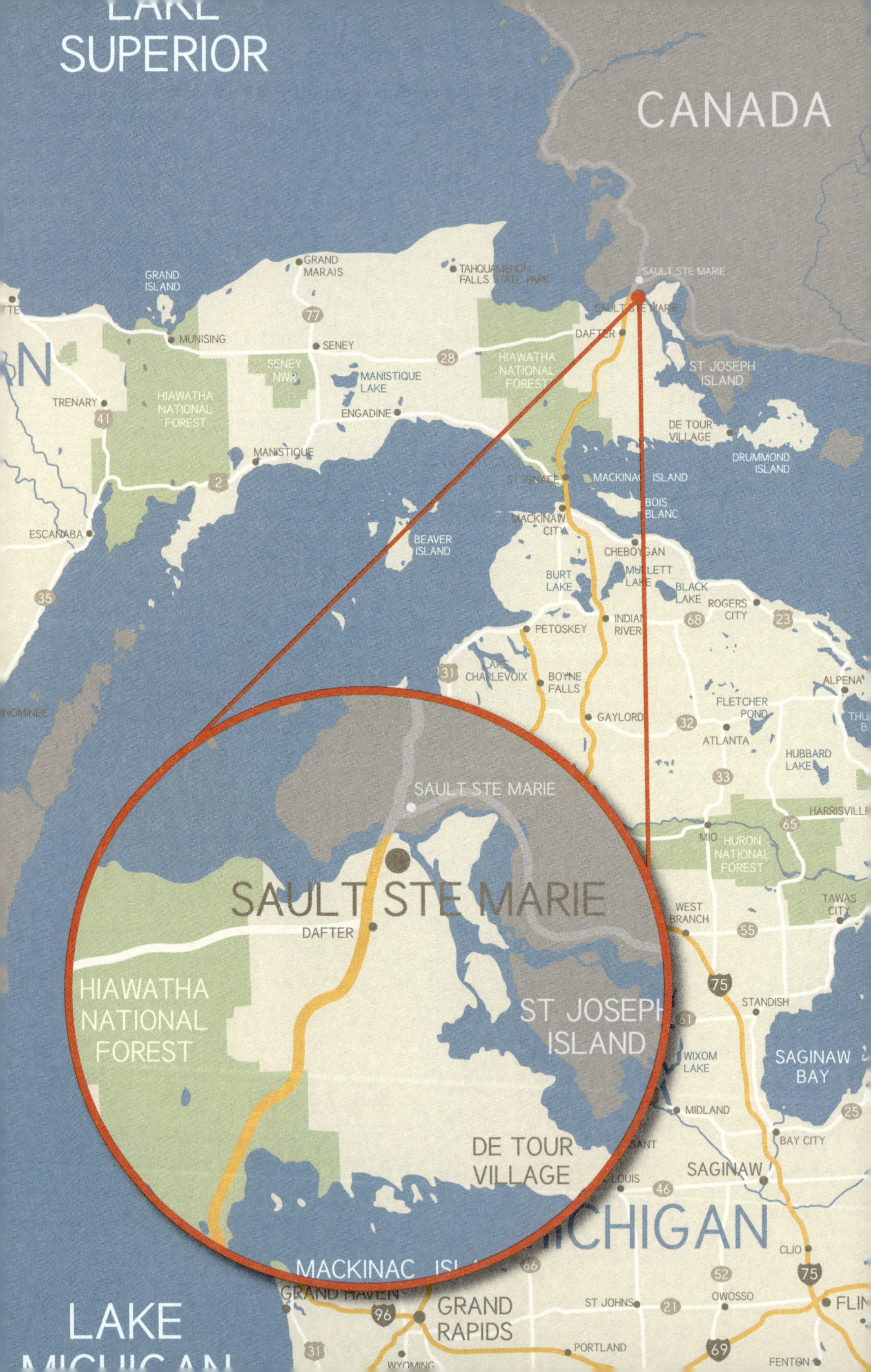
SUPERIOR
CANADA
GRAND ISLAND
GRAND MARAIS
TAHQUAMENON FALLS STATE PARK
SAULT STE MARIE
SAULT STE MARIE
MUNISING
SENEY
DAFTER
77
28
SENEY NWR
MANISTIQUE LAKE
HIAWATHA NATIONAL FOREST
HIAWATHA NATIONAL FOREST
ST JOSEPH ISLAND
TRENARY
41
ENGADINE
DE TOUR VILLAGE
MANISTIQUE
2
DRUMMOND ISLAND
ST IGNACE
MACKINAC ISLAND
BOIS BLANC
ESCANABA
MACKINAW CITY
BEAVER ISLAND
CHEBOYGAN
BURT LAKE
MULLETT LAKE
BLACK LAKE
ROGERS CITY
35
PETOSKEY
INDIAN RIVER
68
23
31
LAKE CHARLEVOIX
BOYNE FALLS
ALPENA
FLETCHER POND
GAYLORD
32
ATLANTA
HUBBARD LAKE
33
MIO
HURON NATIONAL FOREST
65
TAWAS CITY
WEST BRANCH
55
75
STANDISH
61
WIXOM LAKE
SAGINAW BAY
MIDLAND
25
BAY CITY
SAGINAW
46
CLIO
66
52
75
OWOSSO
ST JOHNS
21
96
GRAND RAPIDS
PORTLAND
31
69
WYOMING
FENTON
LAKE
SAULT STE MARIE
SAULT STE MARIE
DAFTER
HIAWATHA NATIONAL FOREST
ISLAND
DE TOUR VILLAGE

SAULT STE. MARIE

LONG OCCUPIED BY the Ojibwa nation, French Jesuit missionaries reached this spot in the UP, where Lake Superior narrows into the St. Mary's River, in the 17th century. When they erected a new settlement called Sault Sainte Marie in 1668, they gave birth to Michigan's oldest city and one of the oldest settled cities in the US.

Sault Ste. Marie is best known for its importance in Great Lakes shipping. In 1885, the first of the city's six Soo Locks was constructed to permit traffic to Lake Huron and beyond. And while the locks were built for economic reasons, they have proven to be so fascinating that an estimated 500,000 people visit each year to observe, tour, and cruise through them. Travelers also enjoy Sault Ste. Marie for its Lake Superior access, its numerous opportunities for year-round outdoor recreation, and its easy access to Canada. Sault Ste. Marie, Ontario, sits just across the St. Mary's River from Sault Ste. Marie, Michigan, via the graceful Sault Ste. Marie International Bridge. Don't forget your passport!

Soo Locks

209 E Portage Ave. • 906-253-9453 • saultstemarie.com/attractions/soo-locks

Within months of the completion of the first of **Sault Ste. Marie**'s locks in the mid-1850s, it had become a tourist attraction. By 1880, there had already developed a canal-side park with footpaths, viewing benches, and a decorative fountain. The park remains, and you can watch passing ships during their March to January sailing season. In the summer months, the locks' visitor center and its observation deck is a good choice. The center's exhibits highlight the size of this engineering marvel, which annually transports 86 million tons of freight aboard 7,000 ships over the 21-foot height difference between Lakes Superior and Huron.

The **Soo Locks Boat Tour** provides an opportunity to sail along the Sault Ste. Marie waterfront and through the locks for a close-up look. Visitors can also join in on Engineers Day, held annually in late June, a rare opportunity for the visiting public to walk through and observe firsthand this engineering feat.

Soo Locks (Courtesy of Sault Ste Marie CVB)

Tower of History (Courtesy of Sault Ste Marie CVB)

Tower of History

326 E Portage Ave. • 906-632-3658 • saulthistoricsites.com/tower-of-history

The Tower of History soars above the city of **Sault Ste. Marie**, a 210-foot, 25-story structure in an area where high-rises are unknown. The tower was constructed in 1968 by the Catholic Church as the Shrine of the Missionaries, paying homage to the city's Jesuit founders, among others. But the project never really took off, and instead, the city unveiled the Tower of History in 1980.

The tower's ground floor provides a timeline of the region's history, including the role of French missionaries in Sault Ste. Marie. Exhibits in the Tower of History reach back to explore the history of Native Americans in the area, and they cover the more recent past as well, covering the years after the missionary era. After viewing the historical displays, ascend the tower via elevator or 292 stairs for spectacular bird's-eye views of the **Soo Locks** and, on a clear day, up to 1,200 miles beyond.

The Antlers

804 E Portage Ave. • 906-253-1728 • saultantlers.com

✓ A beloved landmark in **Sault Ste. Marie**, the Antlers features a decor chock-a-block with taxidermied animals. Across the restaurant's ceiling and walls hang more than 200 mounts, from fish to moose, and from otters to bears and lions. The collection has amassed over more than 60 years and continues to grow, acquired through the owners' bartering skills, from families who donate unwanted taxidermies and occasionally from hungry patrons in exchange for free food.

The Antlers began its life as a saloon, the **Bucket of Blood**. During Prohibition, the business ostensibly took up selling ice cream but was busted when authorities discovered the alcohol sales going on in a back room. These days, the Antlers has become a legitimate family favorite. The menu's signature entrée is its half-pound hamburgers that you can order with a side of poutine or chili cheese fries. Wild game, barbecue, and local fish platters are also satisfyingly good.

The Antlers (Courtesy of Sault Ste Marie CVB)

Nearby Alternatives

Museum: Museum Ship *Valley Camp*

Walk through a Great Lakes freighter and you'll grasp precisely how large these ships are. That's the experience you can expect aboard the *Valley Camp*. In addition to viewing the retired ship's quarters, you'll see a Great Lakes aquarium, museum exhibits related to lakers, and an impressive display of *Edmund Fitzgerald* artifacts, including two surviving lifeboats.

501 E Water St.
906-632-3658
saulthistoricsites.com/museum-ship-valley-camp

Outdoors: The I-500

In early February, all of **Sault Ste. Marie** gathers for the I-500, one of the world's most grueling races: a 500-mile snowmobile circuit around an ice track, at speeds exceeding 100 mph. Casual snowmobilers flock to Sault Ste. Marie in winter, where 200 miles of sled trails take advantage of 120 inches of snowfall annually.

984 E 4th St.
906-635-1500
I-500.com

Discover: Point Iroquois Lighthouse

The Point Iroquois Lighthouse, its structure painted white and topped by a brilliant red roof, sits high above Lake Superior where it narrows to enter the **St. Mary's River**. In warm weather, visitors can climb the tower and tour the lighthouse-keeping museum. The grounds are open year-round.

12942 W Lakeshore Dr., Brimley
906-437-5272

Tour: Agawa Canyon Train Tour

Grab your passport and head across the Sault Ste. Marie International Bridge to Ontario for a daylong Canadian adventure through the Agawa Canyon. The 10-hour train trip takes visitors through mixed forest, alongside crystal-clear lakeshores, over trestle bridges, and through rugged canyons inaccessible via car.

87 Huron St., Sault Ste. Marie, Ontario
844-246-9458
agawatrain.com

Trip Planning

Sault Ste. Marie Convention & Visitors Bureau

225 E Portage Ave.
906-632-3366
saultstemarie.com

GRAND ISLAND
GRAND MARAIS
TAHQUAMENON FALLS STATE PARK
SAULT STE MARIE
MUNISING
SENEY
SENEY NWR
MANISTIQUE LAKE
HIAWATHA NATIONAL FOREST
DAFTER
ST JOSEPH ISLAND
TRENARY
ENGADINE
DE TOUR VILLAGE
MANISTIQUE
DRUMMOND ISLAND
ST IGNACE
MACKINAC ISLAND
BOIS BLANC
ESCANABA
MACKINAW CITY
BEAVER ISLAND
CHEBOYGAN
MULLETT LAKE
BURT LAKE
BLACK LAKE
ROGERS CITY
PETOSKEY
INDIAN RIVER
LAKE CHARLEVOIX
BOYNE FALLS
MENOMINEE
MANITOU ISLANDS
GAYLORD
FLETCHER POND
TORCH LAKE
ATLANTA
MANCELONA
HUBBARD LAKE
GLEN
ELK RAPIDS
GRAYLING
MIO
HURON NATIONAL FOREST
WEST BRANCH
STANDISH
WIXOM LAKE
SAGINAW BAY
MIDLAND
BAY CITY
SAGINAW
CLIO
OWOSSO
ST JOHNS
PORTLAND
FENTON
LAKE MICHIGAN
LANSING
HOLLAND
SAUGATUCK
HASTINGS
CHARLOTTE
ALLEGAN
ANN ARBOR
SOUTH HAVEN
BATTLE CREEK
KALAMAZOO
JACKSON
MICHIGAN

MACKINAC ISLAND

SET WITHIN THE Straits of Mackinac, between Michigan's Upper and Lower Peninsulas and within view of the Mackinac Bridge, Mackinac Island is a perennially popular vacation destination. Having banned cars since 1896, the island is explored by foot, bicycle, and horse carriage, which naturally relaxes the pace of life. Once you've arrived by ferry or plane from **St. Ignace** or **Mackinaw City**, you'll spend your days skipping stones in Lake Huron, bicycling, shopping for fudge and resort wear, and watching the sunset from the front porch of a B&B.

Although Mackinac Island is a popular family and romantic getaway, there is plenty of history on this island. The Anishnaabek people enjoyed a long history on the island, followed by French explorers and missionaries in the 17th century and American and British forces in the 1800s. A visit to Mackinac Island allows opportunities to explore American history as well as the joys of island life.

Mackinac Island is primarily a summer destination, but it's possible to visit in winter. Arrive by plane, then snowshoe and cross-country ski across a thick blanket of snow amid the quiet.

Mackinac Island Carriage Tours

7278 Main St.
906-847-3307
mict.com

You're never far from the *clip-clop* of horse hooves on Mackinac Island. While much of this island is easily reached on foot or by bicycle, horse carriages are utilized for tasks ranging from transporting hotel guests' luggage to hauling trash and delivering drywall for a summer cottage restoration.

Mackinac Island Carriage Tours also offers sightseeing tours of Mackinac Island by horse carriage, and has been since 1869, making this the world's oldest horse-and-buggy service. The company operates 100 carriages and stables 400 horses on the island, putting them to use on public tours that last nearly two hours. The route begins downtown and travels past the Wings of Mackinac Butterfly Conservatory, Arch Rock, Skull Cave, Fort Holmes, the Michigan Governor's Mansion, Fort Mackinac, and the Grand Hotel, with stops along the way. Mackinac Island Carriage Tours also offers private customizable tours and taxi service.

Mackinac Island Carriage Tours (Courtesy of Mackinac Island Tourism Bureau)

Fort Mackinac (Courtesy of Mackinac State Historic Parks)

Fort Mackinac

Fort St. • 231-436-4100 • mackinacparks.com

Set high on a bluff overlooking the **Straits of Mackinac** and downtown Mackinac Island, Fort Mackinac dates from the late 1700s and once served as a key military post in the Great Lakes. Thirteen fort structures recall life at the fort in the 18th and 19th centuries, including officers' quarters, a hospital, and military drills. The fort's cannon fires multiple times daily, a boom heard throughout the island. After touring the fort, stay for a meal at the **Fort Mackinac Island Tea Room** in the historic Officers' Stone Quarters, Michigan's oldest building, from 1780. The restaurant serves salads and sandwiches and enjoys some of the finest views of any restaurant in Michigan.

Admission to Fort Mackinac includes entrance to the **Manoogian Mackinac Art Museum**, the **Biddle House Native American Museum**, and several additional historic house museums downtown. Ask about a combination ticket if you plan to visit additional **Mackinac State Historic Parks**.

Bistro on the Greens

6633 Main St. • 906-847-3000 • missionpoint.com/restaurants

Mediterranean-inspired food and creative craft cocktails fill the menu at Bistro on the Greens, a restaurant at Mackinac Island's Mission Point Resort. After an afternoon of beachcombing, bicycling, and golfing, dig into summertime favorites like hearty burgers, crisp salads, flatbreads, and paninis, or choose from entrees such as fresh local whitefish or lake trout, salmon, or steak. Top it off with a Michigan cherry profiterole.

The menu at Bistro on the Greens is fresh, satisfying, and tailored to Michigan summers. But the restaurant's setting is also a winner. Dining is almost exclusively outdoors, beneath sunny yellow umbrella tables set up on a broad wooden deck. While you dine, enjoy the tidily manicured **Greens of Mackinac** putting course, with its brilliant flower beds and attractive water features. And beyond the lawns are the Straits of Mackinac where, if you're lucky, you'll be able to watch freighters passing by.

Bistro on the Greens
(Courtesy of Mission Point Resort)

Nearby Alternatives

Museum: Richard & Jane Manoogian Mackinac Art Museum

An extraordinary collection of Mackinac-related art fills the galleries at this museum, set within the walls of the federal government's 1838 Indian Dormitory. Hand-beaded Native American garments from the 17th century and maps from the 18th century share space with Mackinac Island souvenirs of the Victorian era, vintage Grand Hotel photographs, and contemporary watercolor landscapes.

7070 Main St.
906-847-3328
mackinacparks.com

Activity: M-185

You'll find 1,400 bicycles on **Mackinac Island**, at rental shops on Main St. and resorts like **Grand Hotel and Mission Point**. Take a spin along the eight-mile perimeter of the island, along M-185. The flat route leads from the downtown past pebbly beaches, **Mackinac Bridge** vistas, charming summer cottages, and **Arch Rock**.

Lake Shore Dr./Main St.

Venue: Grand Hotel

Grand Hotel has been a Mackinac Island landmark since 1887. Guest rooms are each decorated in vibrant, one-of-a-kind fashion, fine dining restaurants feature impeccably trained staff, and original art appears around every corner. Non-guests can self-tour the historic hotel for a fee, enjoy a drink on the world's longest porch, and explore the lush gardens surrounding the Grand.

286 Grand Ave.
906-847-3331
grandhotel.com

Activity: The Jewel

Grand Hotel's premier golf course is the Jewel. The 18-hole course is divided into the **Grand Nine**, near the hotel and overlooking the Straits of Mackinac, and the Woods Nine, in the island's interior. A 15-minute carriage ride connects the two, making the Jewel the only course in the country with horse carriage service.

286 Grand Ave.
906-847-9218
grandhotel.com

Trip Planning

Mackinac Island Tourism Bureau

7274 Main St.
906-847-3783
mackinacisland.org

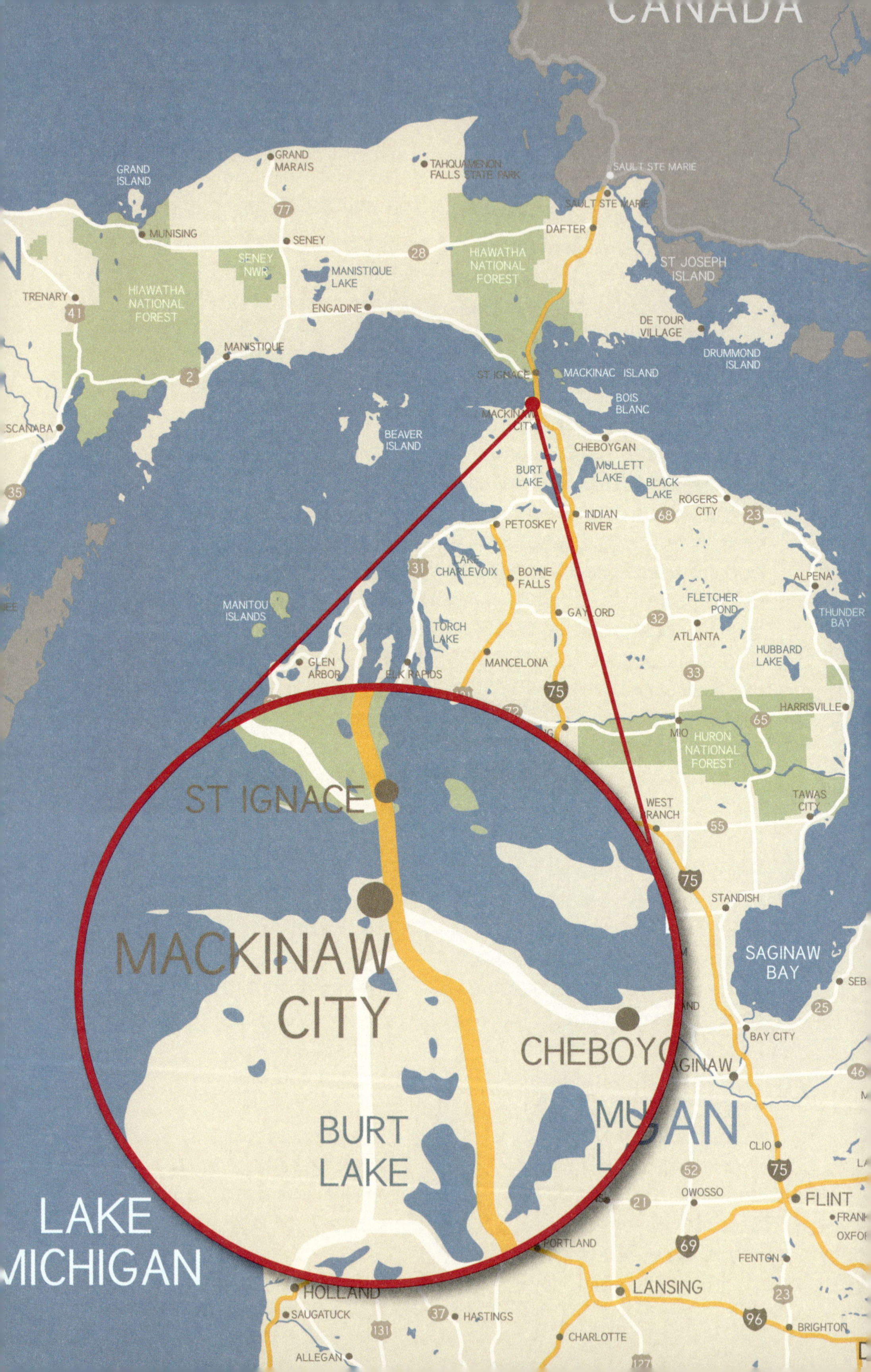
CANADA
GRAND ISLAND
GRAND MARAIS
TAHQUAMENON FALLS STATE PARK
SAULT STE MARIE
SAULT STE MARIE
MUNISING
SENEY
DAFTER
SENEY NWR
MANISTIQUE LAKE
HIAWATHA NATIONAL FOREST
ST JOSEPH ISLAND
TRENARY
HIAWATHA NATIONAL FOREST
ENGADINE
DE TOUR VILLAGE
MANISTIQUE
DRUMMOND ISLAND
ST IGNACE
MACKINAC ISLAND
BOIS BLANC
MACKINAW CITY
BEAVER ISLAND
CHEBOYGAN
BURT LAKE
MULLETT LAKE
BLACK LAKE
ROGERS CITY
PETOSKEY
INDIAN RIVER
LAKE CHARLEVOIX
BOYNE FALLS
ALPENA
FLETCHER POND
MANITOU ISLANDS
GAYLORD
THUNDER BAY
ATLANTA
TORCH LAKE
HUBBARD LAKE
GLEN ARBOR
MANCELONA
ELK RAPIDS
HARRISVILLE
MIO
HURON NATIONAL FOREST
ST IGNACE
TAWAS CITY
WEST BRANCH
STANDISH
MACKINAW CITY
SAGINAW BAY
CHEBOYG
BAY CITY
SAGINAW
BURT LAKE
CLIO
FLINT
OWOSSO
LAKE MICHIGAN
PORTLAND
FENTON
LANSING
HOLLAND
SAUGATUCK
HASTINGS
BRIGHTON
CHARLOTTE
ALLEGAN

MACKINAW CITY

MACKINAW CITY SITS at a crossroads, one it has occupied since before recorded time. Located at the confluence of two Great Lakes and the near joining of the Upper and Lower Peninsulas, the Straits of Mackinac has long served as an exchange point for commerce and cultures.

There is much to draw modern travelers to Mackinaw City, beginning with its unique and beautiful landscape. Boaters, hikers, and campers find plenty of Great Lakes' shoreline to explore. History buffs pore over Native American, French, and British artifacts at historic parks and forts. And those who love shopping and high-end dining head to downtown Mackinaw City or board the local ferry for **Mackinac Island** resorts. Last but never least, the **Mackinac Bridge** beckons travelers, with its graceful white span in the daylight, and with a thousand glimmering lights after dark.

The French and British both left their mark on the Straits, in the landscape and the language. The French wrote the word "Mackinac," the British "Mackinaw." Either way, the pronunciation is the same, with the sound of a final "w."

Mackinac Bridge

I-75 • 906-643-7600 • mackinacbridge.org

✓ The Mackinac Bridge is so synonymous with northern Michigan, many Michiganders simply refer to her as "The Bridge." When it was completed in 1957, Michigan became physically united for the first time. Previously, residents had to rely on ferry service between the Upper and Lower Peninsulas.

Driving across the "Mighty Mac" offers thrilling views of the five-mile Straits of Mackinac. The thrill is even greater on Labor Day, the only day of the year when the State of Michigan allows pedestrians to join in a Bridge Walk. The experience is sometimes chilly, often windy, and always memorable.

The bright white of the Mackinac Bridge contrasts brilliantly with its backdrop of deep blue sky and water, making this span a perennial favorite of photographers. For the best photo ops, visit **Lighthouse Park**, near the tip of the Lower Peninsula, or **Straits State Park**, on the UP side.

Mackinac Bridge (Courtesy of Mackinac State Historic Parks)

Fort Michilimackinac (Courtesy of Amy S. Eckert)

Colonial Michilimackinac

102 W Straits Ave. • 231-436-4100 • mackinacparks.com

Established in the early 18th century, frequented by Native American traders, European missionaries, and voyageurs, occupied first by the French, later by the British, and now by Americans, Colonial Michilimackinac ranks as one of the most important historical sites in Michigan. The military outpost and colonial-era trading center has been carefully re-created as it appeared in 1780 following decades of intense and ongoing archaeological work. Costumed interpreters explain life in the Upper Great Lakes at the time of the American Revolution, and physical and video displays dig deeper, exploring everything from 18th-century kitchen gardens to period weaponry. The fort sits along a beautiful stretch of Lake Michigan, with great Mackinac Bridge views and opportunities to skip stones and play in the water.

Colonial Michilimackinac is open from mid-May to mid-October. Ask about combination tickets for entry to additional **Mackinac State Historic Parks**, including **Old Mackinac Point Lighthouse**, **Historic Mill Creek**, and **Mackinac Island's Fort Mackinac**.

Dixie Saloon

401 E Central Ave. • 231-436-5449 • dixiesaloon.com

The Old Dixie Highway once ran all the way from Miami to Sault Ste. Marie. In Mackinaw City, the highway passed by the Dixie Saloon, established in 1890 to offer food and drink to customers waiting for the ferry to shuttle them across the Straits of Mackinac to the UP.

Today, Dixie Saloon occupies a modern building with a log-cabin vibe near downtown shops and hotels, a half mile from the Mackinac Bridge and an easy walk from Mackinac Island ferries. Given the restaurant's immense size, this restaurant is likely to have space for you when summer crowds overwhelm everyplace else.

Hearty burgers and sandwiches make up most of their menu, but you can also indulge in Great Lakes fish platters, barbecue ribs, and UP-style pasties. Dixie Saloon has a brewery on-site and pours a dozen of their own beers, from IPAs and blondes to a Winterweizen and a Candy Cane Stout.

Dixie Saloon (Courtesy of yksnorb)

Nearby Alternatives

Discover: Old Mackinac Point Lighthouse

Constructed in 1889, this lighthouse signaled to passing ships their journey past the Lower Peninsula's northernmost tip. Old Mackinac Point, built of honey-colored brick and capped with a brilliant red roof, remains an eye-catching sight. In warm weather, you can climb the tower and visit the lighthouse museum.

526 N Huron Ave.
231-436-4100
mackinacparks.com

Outdoors: Historic Mill Creek Discovery Park

Mackinaw City's restored Mill Creek re-creates the Great Lakes 18th-century lumber era. Learn how millwrights operated and how they transformed Michigan, and then have some modern-day fun on a 50-foot climbing tower, a zip line, and a forest canopy bridge. The park is open from mid-May through Labor Day.

9001 US-23, Cheboygan
231-436-4100
mackinacparks.com

Outdoors: Straits State Park

Set at the northern terminus of the **Mackinac Bridge**, Straits State Park is one of the area's most popular state parks. Visitors can stop in to snap pics, walk the shoreline, catch unsurpassed views of the bridge, or overnight at one of 270 modern campsites.

720 Church St., St. Ignace
906-643-8620
michigandnr.com/parksandtrails

Museum: Museum of Ojibwa Culture

The historic grounds of the **French Jesuit Mission** comprise the Museum of Ojibwa Culture. The history, culture, and folklore of the native Ojibwa are presented here through physical and digital displays and a longhouse. Check out the excellent Ojibwa-made gift shop and the grave of Father Jacques Marquette, still venerated by the local Ojibwa.

500 N State St., St. Ignace
906-643-9161
museumofojibwaculture.net

Trip Planning

Mackinaw Area Visitors Bureau

10800 W US-23
231-436-5664
mackinawcity.com

GRAND ISLAND
MARQUETTE
MUNISING
GRAND MARAIS
SENEY
TAHQUAMENON FALLS STATE PARK
SAULT STE MARIE
SAULT STE MARIE
DAFTER
HIGAN
TRENARY
HIAWATHA NATIONAL FOREST
SENEY NWR
MANISTIQUE LAKE
ENGADINE
HIAWATHA NATIONAL FOREST
ST JOSEP ISLAND
DE TOUR VILLAGE
MANISTIQUE
ST IGNACE
MACKINAC ISLAND
BOIS BLANC
NORWAY
ESCANABA
MACKINAW CITY
BEAVER ISLAND
CHEBOYGAN
BURT LAKE
MULLETT LAKE
BLACK LAKE
ROGERS CITY
PETOSKEY
INDIAN RIVER
LAKE CHARLEVOIX
BOYNE FALLS
MENOMINEE
MANITOU ISLANDS
GAYLORD
TORCH LAKE
ATLANTA
GLEN ARBOR
ELK RAPIDS
MANCELONA
TRAVERSE CITY
GRAYLING
MIO
FRANKFORT
GREEN BAY
BEAR LAKE
MESICK
WEST BRANCH
CADILLAC
HOUGHTON LAKE
HARRISON
EVART
CLARE
WIXOM LAKE
MIDLAND
MT PLEASANT
ST LOUIS
SAGINA
CHIGAN
ST JOHNS
OWOSS
PORTLAND
LANSING
CHARLOTTE
BATTLE CREEK
JACKSON
BENTON HARBOR
JONESVILLE
BURT LAKE
PETOSKEY
INDIA RIVER
BOYNE FALLS

PETOSKEY

PETOSKEY OCCUPIES A magnificent piece of real estate: the sparkling waters of Lake Michigan's Little Traverse Bay to the north, a 38-mile chain of inland lakes to the east, and rolling hills and still more inland lakes to the south and west. And the area's temperate location means comfortable temps in summer and thick layers of snow in winter.

All of that makes the Petoskey area a popular travel destination. In spring, carpets of pink and white trilliums brighten the forest floor. In summer, the area's numerous golf courses burst into lush greens. Sailboats and cruisers splash in the Lake Michigan surf, and beachcombers gather up buckets of Michigan's state stone, the Petoskey stone. Fall turns the surrounding forest brilliant shades of red and yellow. And when winter arrives, the region's three ski resorts swing into action.

Tourism in Petoskey may well trace its roots to Bay View, a Chautauqua-style summer camp founded by Methodists in 1875. That community continues today, offering concerts and educational lectures to all and fostering a regional interest in art and culture.

Boyne Mountain Resort

1 Boyne Mountain Rd., Boyne Falls • 855-688-7024 • boynemountain.com

✓ Boyne Mountain Resort opened in 1947 with two ski runs, a used chairlift, and a small warming hut. More than 75 years later, the resort ranks as one of Michigan's finest. Alpine skiers and boarders can schuss over 415 acres of terrain and down 60 runs. More than 35 kilometers of groomed and dedicated cross-country ski and snowshoe trails crisscross Boyne, and winter sports enthusiasts can also go horseback riding, fat-tire biking, skating, and tubing. In summer, Boyne Mountain offers bike trails, swimming and paddling on **Deer Lake**, disc golf, and two 18-hole championship golf courses, the Alpine and the Monument. No matter the weather, visitors can walk across **SkyBridge Michigan**, the world's longest timber-towered suspension bridge, or splash around in **Avalanche Bay**, an indoor waterpark with 88,000 square feet of activities. And there are cabins, a villa, and lodges to overnight in, as well as on-site shopping and dining.

Boyne Mountain Resort (Courtesy of Boyne Mountain Resort)

Bay Harbor Golf Club (Courtesy of Inn at Bay Harbor, Autograph Collection)

Bay Harbor Golf Club

5800 Coastal Ridge Dr., Bay Harbor • 231-439-4028 • bayharborgolf.com

With more than 30 golf courses within a 20-mile drive of Petoskey, golfers have a wealth of riches to choose from when they're ready to tee up. The Bay Harbor Golf Club ranks among the area's best and most scenic courses. Located within the lakeshore community of Bay Harbor, just west of Petoskey, which offers shopping, dining, cultural activities, and residential and tourist lodging, the golf course ranks as a key local attraction and is open to the public.

The Bay Harbor Golf Club is set partially within an abandoned shale quarry and partially along a beautiful stretch of Lake Michigan shore, where unpredictable winds can challenge play. Golf course architect Arthur Hills designed Bay Harbor with 27 holes divided among three distinct courses: **Links, Quarry, and Preserve**. Golfers typically play the courses in pairs, to balance lakeshore and inland terrain and to create three unique golfing experiences.

City Park Grill

432 E Lake St. • 231-347-0101 • cityparkgrill.com

☑ McCarty Hall opened for business in downtown Petoskey in 1875 promising billiards, cigars, and booze in a male-only establishment. When Prohibition hit Michigan in 1917, tales of underground tunnels, alcohol raids, and ghost sightings made the restaurant legendary. But it was the patronage of Ernest Hemingway that really put the establishment now known as the City Park Grill on the map. The author vacationed at his nearby summer cottage in the 1910s and '20s and headed to this restaurant to watch bare-knuckle boxing in the neighboring park and jot down short stories and books from his favorite barstool. Hemingway fans still like to visit the City Park Grill, paying homage to their author at his favorite hangout.

Besides the City Park Grill's notable history, its interior draws attention with a 32-foot solid mahogany bar and a menu of sandwiches, burgers, hand-cut steaks, chops, and Great Lakes whitefish.

City Park Grill (Courtesy of Petoskey Area Visitors Bureau)

Nearby Alternatives

Tour: Earl Young Mushroom Houses

Self-taught architect Earl Young launched his building career in 1919, using free-form, undulating lines and organic materials like local limestone and boulders to construct his "Mushroom Houses." The 26 residences and four commercial properties often appear to grow out of the earth or melt into it. Tour the buildings on foot or by car using an online map.

103 State St., Charlevoix
231-547-0373
chxhistory.com

Outdoors: Tunnel of Trees

Michigan's M-119 traces the contours of **Little Traverse Bay**, leading north out of Petoskey toward **Harbor Springs**. There, the route narrows into the Tunnel of Trees, a serpentine drive through hardwoods and along a bluff overlooking Lake Michigan. Considered one of Michigan's most scenic drives, the route is especially beautiful during spring wildflower and fall foliage seasons.

M-119

Shopping: Gaslight District

Petoskey's downtown, called the Gaslight District to emphasize its history, is one of Michigan's most charming shopping destinations. Favorites include **McLean & Eakin**, an independent bookstore; **Grandpa Shorter's**, with Michigan-themed food gifts and souvenirs; **Harbor Wear** for resort clothing; and **Northgoods**, selling Petoskey stone art, jewelry, and housewares.

E. Lake St. at Howard St.
petoskeydowntown.com

Outdoors: Magnus City Park Beach

Michigan's state stone, the Petoskey stone, is a gray, fossilized, 350-million-year-old coral that is most commonly found in this corner of the state. Head to Magnus City Park and take a squirt bottle with you, as the stone's telltale hexagonal pattern is only visible when the stones are wet.

901 W Lake St.
231-347-1027

Trip Planning

Petoskey Area Visitors Bureau
401 E Mitchell St.
231-348-2755
petoskeyarea.com

CANADA
ALPENA
THUNDER BAY
HUBBARD LAKE
GRAND ISLAND
MANITOU ISLANDS
TORCH LAKE
GLEN ARBOR
ELK RAPIDS
MANCELONA
GAYLORD
FLETCHER POND
ATLANTA
HUBBARD LAKE
THUNDER BAY
TRAVERSE CITY
GRAYLING
MIO
HURON NATIONAL FOREST
HARRISVILLE
FRANKFORT
BEAR LAKE
MESICK
CADILLAC
HOUGHTON LAKE
WEST BRANCH
TAWAS CITY
MANISTEE
STANDISH
HARRISON
LUDINGTON
REED CITY
EVART
CLARE
WIXOM LAKE
SAGINAW BAY
SEBEWAING
BALDWIN
MANISTEE NATIONAL FOREST
SILVER LAKE SAND DUNES
SHELBY
BIG RAPIDS
MIDLAND
MT PLEASANT
BAY CITY
WHITE CLOUD
ST LOUIS
SAGINAW
MARLETTE
HOWARD CITY
MICHIGAN
MUSKEGON
CLIO
LAPEER
GRAND HAVEN
GRAND RAPIDS
ST JOHNS
OWOSSO
FLINT
FRANKENMUTH
OXFORD
PORTLAND

ALPENA

THIS CITY OF about 10,000 sits in the protected curve of Thunder Bay, tucked away from the wide-open expanse of Lake Huron. Alpena is a place that sailors seek, a safe harbor from the mighty storms that can plague the Great Lakes. Mariners from prehistoric times to the present have headed to Alpena when the weather threatens.

The sanctuary continues to draw travelers to this corner of northeast Michigan. The area's golden beaches, lighthouses, forest preserves, and boat launches are more peaceful than other more crowded areas in Michigan. Hotels and restaurants have a casual feel and are unlikely to require reservations. Alpena offers the solitude and quiet craved by so many travelers, particularly those from urban areas.

Make time to visit **Thunder Bay National Marine Sanctuary** and its **Great Lakes Maritime Heritage Center**. But don't miss the other charms that Alpena has to offer. The **Besser Museum** offers a mix of history, art, and science as well as the only planetarium in northern Michigan. And Alpena's local parks and waterways offer lots of natural respite.

Great Lakes Maritime Heritage Center

500 W Fletcher St. • 989-884-6200
thunderbay.noaa.gov

☑ The Great Lakes Maritime Heritage Center houses the Thunder Bay National Marine Sanctuary's visitor center and serves as the sanctuary's de facto headquarters. But the heritage center also includes a free museum with exhibits that revolve around Thunder Bay and extend to the geology of Michigan's northeastern Lower Peninsula. It's a stop worth making, even if you have no intention of checking out the wrecks preserved by the underwater sanctuary in **Alpena's Thunder Bay**. (Although you should check out the wrecks preserved by the underwater sanctuary.)

The museum's displays are extensive and span centuries, from early Native American navigation of the waterways to the dramatic 18th- and 19th-century wrecks in nearby **Shipwreck Alley** and contemporary Great Lakes navigation. Information about local shipwrecks is conveyed through interactive displays. You can also walk the deck of a re-created ship as a simulated storm approaches, climb inside Native American vessels, and even try your hand at tying nautical knots.

Great Lakes Maritime Heritage Center (Courtesy of Amy S. Eckert)

Thunder Bay National Marine Sanctuary (Courtesy of Tane Casserley, NOAA)

Thunder Bay National Marine Sanctuary

500 W Fletcher St. • 989-884-6200 • thunderbay.noaa.gov

Nearly 100 shipwrecks lie silently beneath the cold waters of Thunder Bay, the broad harbor that hugs the shores of Alpena. From Civil War–era steamers to 20th-century schooners, from wooden tugboats to passenger ships and early steel freighters, the wrecks that lie within Alpena's Shipwreck Alley are preserved within the Thunder Bay National Marine Sanctuary, the only freshwater sanctuary in the US.

While these vessels have been lost beneath the icy waves of Lake Huron, the ships' stories still have the power to fascinate, and oftentimes their remains are still accessible to modern-day visitors. You can see these century-old wrecks via glass-bottom boat tours, which go out regularly during the warm-weather months from the visitor center within the **Great Lakes Maritime Heritage Center**. You can also snorkel, kayak, or stand-up paddleboard (SUP) over shallow wrecks like the *Portland* and the *Albany*. Contact the visitor center for printed directions.

Austin Brothers Beer Co.

821 W Miller St. • 989-340-2300 • austinbrosbeerco.com

✓ Brant and Blake Austin, the owners of Austin Brothers Beer, were natives of Southern California when they discovered Alpena on a cross-country road trip. The family instantly fell in love with the Lake Huron city, and with no other ties to northern Michigan, quit their jobs, packed up their families, and relocated to Alpena, where they opened this popular microbrewery near Lake Besser.

Austin Brothers serves lunch, dinner, and late-night bar snacks. A lengthy menu of hearty sandwiches, burgers, pitas, soups, and salads are smoked, grilled, and cooked in-house with locally sourced ingredients. Naturally, it's the Austin Brothers' beer that draws most people. The offerings change seasonally and include everything from IPAs and amber ales to sours and fruit beers. Austin Brothers also serves beer cocktails, including shandies and mixes of two draft beers, like the Cherralyzer, a blend of imperial IPA and cherry beer.

Austin Brothers Beer (Courtesy of Amy S. Eckert)

Nearby Alternatives

Museum: Besser Museum

Science, history, art, and the natural world come together in the Besser Museum. Taxidermied wildlife detail the animal and fish you might find outdoors, and the **LaFarge Fossil Park** out back allows visitors to hunt for and keep any fossils they find. The museum is also home to northern Michigan's only planetarium.

491 Johnson St.
989-356-2202
bessermuseum.org

Discover: Presque Isle Lighthouses

Three remarkable lighthouses occupy Presque Isle: New Presque Isle Lighthouse (1870), the tallest on the Great Lakes that the public may climb; Old Presque Isle Lighthouse (1840), one of the Great Lakes' oldest; and the **Harbor Range Light** (1870), dedicated to female lighthouse keepers. There is also a **Keeper's House Museum** (1905).

4500 E Grand Lake Rd.
989-787-0814
presqueislelighthouses.org

Outdoors: Ocqueoc Falls

The largest waterfall in Michigan's Lower Peninsula sits along the Ocqueoc River. Splash and play in the water, which is reached by the fully accessible Ocqueoc Falls Bicentennial Pathway, or fish for trout and steelhead. The Ocqueoc Falls State Forest Campground offers 13 rustic campsites on a first come, first served basis.

M-68, Rogers City
989-734-2543
michigandnr.com/parksandtrails

Outdoors: Thompson's Harbor State Park

Because Alpena's remoteness makes stargazing a natural, Thompson's Harbor State Park is home to one of Michigan's **Dark Sky Parks**. The quiet seven-mile stretch of Lake Huron beach lacks virtually any light pollution, ideal for summertime viewing. The park is largely undeveloped and popular with cross-country skiers, mountain bikers, hikers, and anglers.

US-23, Rogers City
989-734-2543
michigandnr.com/parksandtrails

Trip Planning

Alpena Area Convention & Visitors Bureau

420 N 2nd Ave.
989-340-2288
visitalpena.com

MANISTIQUE LAKE
NATIONAL FOREST
ST JOSEPH ISLAND
HIAWATHA NATIONAL FOREST
ENGADINE
MANISTIQUE
DE TOUR VILLAGE
DRUMMOND ISLAND
ST IGNACE
MACKINAC ISLAND
BOIS BLANC
MACKINAW CITY
BEAVER ISLAND
CHEBOYGAN
MULLETT LAKE
BURT LAKE
BLACK LAKE
ROGERS CITY
INDIAN RIVER
PETOSKEY
LAKE CHARLEVOIX
BOYNE FALLS
ALPENA
FLETCHER POND
THUNDER BAY
MANITOU ISLANDS
GAYLORD
ATLANTA
TORCH LAKE
HUBBARD LAKE
GLEN ARBOR
ELK RAPIDS
MANCELONA
TRAVERSE CITY
HARRISVILLE
GRAYLING
MIO
HURON NATIONAL FOREST
FRANKFORT
TAWAS CITY
WEST BRANCH
BEAR LAKE
MESICK
CADILLAC
HOUGHTON LAKE
MANISTEE
STANDISH
HARRISON
LUDINGTON
EVART
CLARE
WIXOM LAKE
SAGINAW BAY
SEBEWAING
MIDLAND
BAY CITY
SAGINAW
MARLETT
CLIO
LAPEER
FLINT
FRANKENMUTH
OXFORD
FENTON
BRIGHTON
ANN ARBOR
DEARBORN
JACKSON
COLDWATER
ADRIAN
MONROE
HUDSON
NILES
SOUTH BEND
GAYLORD
ATLANTA
41
2
68
23
31
32
33
75
131
72
22
65
66
37
55
61
10
25
46
96
223
75
32
33

GAYLORD

THE SMALL TOWN of Gaylord packs a punch when it comes to travel and tourism. Only about 4,000 people live here year-round. But the city lies at the heart of Michigan's best golf region. The area's dense hardwood forests and hilly landscape make Gaylord a prime spot for skiing, too, oftentimes at resorts that focus on golf in the summer. And because one of the nation's busiest interstates, I-75, runs right through Gaylord, the resort community enjoys easy access.

In the 1930s, Gaylord's Otsego Ski Club encouraged the city to adopt an alpine ski theme in its community architecture to support and enhance the area's reputation as a ski destination. It took several decades for the idea to catch on, but many of Gaylord's buildings sport a charming Swiss look to them.

Head into the hills surrounding Gaylord and you'll discover the area's premier golf courses, commonly called the Gaylord Golf Mecca. Seventeen golf facilities make up the Golf Mecca, many of them designed by top designers like Rees Jones, Robert Trent Jones, and Tom Fazio.

Treetops Resort

3962 Wilkinson Rd. • 866-348-5249 • treetops.com

✓ Treetops Resort, part of the **Gaylord Golf Mecca**, features 81 holes of golf over five award-winning courses inspired and professionally designed by Robert Trent Jones Sr., Tom Fazio, and Rick Smith.

Treetops' Threetops course was the first ever designed by Rick Smith and has been recognized by multiple golf publications as the #1 Par 3 Course in North America. Other courses at Treetops—Premier, the sole Fazio course in Michigan; Signature, Robert Trent Jones's masterpiece, thought to be Michigan's most challenging; and Tradition, Treetops' most player-friendly course—have all gone on to win a handful of their own golf accolades.

In winter, outdoors lovers stow away their golf clubs and pull out their skis. Treetops offers 80 acres of winter terrain, including 24 downhill and snowboard runs, cross-country skiing, snowshoeing, and mushing. Year-round the resort offers accommodations at two lodges, condos, and cottages as well as four restaurants and an ice cream and candy bar.

Treetops Resort (Courtesy of Treetops Resort)

Gaylord Golf Club (Courtesy of Gaylord Golf Mecca)

Gaylord Golf Club

4893 M-32 W • 231-546-3376 • gaylordcountryclub.com

When the Gaylord Country Club (now the Gaylord Golf Club) opened its doors nearly a century ago, there was no such thing as the Gaylord Golf Mecca. The region's first golf course, which was unveiled in 1924 and has occupied its current location since 1975, is now a key member of the **Mecca**, located just west of the town of Gaylord. The 18-hole course is renowned for its excellent course conditions and, because the course is older, its parkland design. Whereas modern courses can take some time to play, this classic course allows a memorable game in less time due to the close proximity of its greens to its tees.

Perhaps most unusual at the Gaylord Golf Club is its status as a semiprivate club, one of few private clubs in northern Michigan that allow public play at any time. Dine at the club's restaurant, the **Grille**, featuring sandwiches, burgers, beer, and wine.

Legends on the Hill

3962 Wilkinson Rd. • 989-732-6711 • treetops.com

Treetops Resort offers multiple memorable outdoor dining experiences. In summer, it's the Beer, Blues, and BBQ Festival and the biweekly Beat the Pro, Meet the Brewery, where contestants match up against a resident golf pro while also sampling the beers of a local microbrewer. In autumn, it's the **Fall Color Tour** and **Progressive Dinner**, with a golf cart ride through the fall foliage and periodic stops for food and Michigan wine tastings. And in winter, it's the Skiable Feast, where participants can ski or snowshoe between five hot food and beverage stops.

For year-round dining, head to **Treetops' Legends on the Hill**. The menu includes standard American fare deliciously prepared—burgers, pizza, barbecue, steak, and fish and chips—as well as a nice selection of craft beers. But the biggest advantage to eating at Legends is its hilltop location. Diners can take in views of the Gaylord countryside, a rolling landscape of hardwood trees particularly beautiful in fall.

Legends on the Hill
(Courtesy of Treetops Resort)

Nearby Alternatives

Discover: Pigeon River Country State Forest Elk Herd

One of the largest, free-ranging elk herds east of the Mississippi River occupies this 114,000-acre state forest. You can see the elk from your car at one of several viewing stations, with the best times being September and October, when the bulls bugle, and April, when the elk actively graze on new spring vegetation.

9984 Twin Lakes Rd., Vanderbilt

pigeonriverdiscoverycenter.org/elk-viewing

Outdoors: Otsego Resort

The vintage ski vibe at Otsego Resort is natural. The ski resort opened its first downhill runs in 1939. Known for its short lift lines, alpine decor, and affordability, Otsego is a favorite destination for families. In addition to downhill skiing and snowboarding, the resort offers snowshoeing trails and tubing runs.

696 M-32 E.

989-732-5181

otsegoclub.com

Outdoors: Sturgeon River Preserve

Two short trails lead through this pleasant stretch along the Sturgeon River, through a thick forest of cedar and hardwoods, and over a boardwalk where the ground becomes swampy. The trail is popular with hikers and allows canoe or kayak access in summer. In winter, head out with your cross-country skis or snowshoes.

3749 Whitmarsh Rd., Vanderbilt, 989-731-0573

headwatersconservancy.org/sturgeon-river-preserve

Restaurant and Brewery: Big Buck Brewery

The operative word at Big Buck Brewery is "big," beginning with the giant beer bottle on the lawn and continuing with a giant antler chandelier and taxidermied elk and deer heads. Along with your big beer, order a burger, steak, or pizza. Big Buck offers one of the largest outdoor patios in Gaylord and regularly features live music.

550 S Wisconsin Ave.

989-448-7072

bigbuckbrewery.com

Trip Planning

Gaylord Travel & Tourism

319 W Main St.

989-732-4000

gaylordmichigan.net

MUNISING
SENEY
DAFTER
SENEY NWR
MANISTIQUE LAKE
HIAWATHA NATIONAL FOREST
HIAWATHA NATIONAL FOREST
ST JOSEPH ISLAND
ENGADINE
DE TOUR VILLAGE
MANISTIQUE
DRUMMOND ISLAND
ST IGNACE
MACKINAC ISLAND
BOIS BLANC
MACKINAW CITY
BEAVER ISLAND
CHEBOYGAN
MULLETT LAKE
BURT LAKE
BLACK LAKE
ROGERS CITY
INDIAN RIVER
PETOSKEY
LAKE CHARLEVOIX
BOYNE FALLS
ALPENA
MANITOU ISLANDS
GAYLORD
FLETCHER POND
THUNDER BAY
TORCH LAKE
ATLANTA
GLEN ARBOR
ELK RAPIDS
MANCELONA
HUBBARD LAKE
TRAVERSE CITY
GRAYLING
HARRISVILLE
MIO
HURON NATIONAL FOREST
FRANKFORT
BEAR LAKE
MESICK
WEST BRANCH
TAWAS CITY
CADILLAC
HOUGHTON LAKE
MANISTEE
STANDISH
HARRISON
WIXOM LAKE
SAGINAW BAY
SEBEWAING
MIDLAND
BAY CITY
MARLET
CLIO
LAPEER
FLINT
OXFORD
FENTON
BRIGHTON
ANN ARBOR
DEARBORN
JACKSON
BENTON HARBOR
JONESVILLE
THREE RIVERS
COLDWATER
ADRIAN
MONROE
HUDSON
NILES
MANITOU ISLANDS
SLEEPING BEAR DUNES NATIONAL LAKESHORE
GLEN ARBOR
22

SLEEPING BEAR DUNES NATIONAL LAKESHORE

THE SLEEPING BEAR Dunes became a national lakeshore in 1970. The popular wilderness area lies 25 miles west of **Traverse City**, with most of the park encompassing a broad swath of sand dunes and hardwood forest on northwest Michigan's mainland. The park includes three campgrounds, multiple swimming beaches, and about 100 miles of trails, which are popular with hikers, backpackers, cross-country skiers, and snowshoers. Also within the park grounds are the North and South Manitou Islands and the ghost town of Glen Haven.

Sleeping Bear Dunes takes its name from Ojibwa legend. The story goes that long ago a mother bear and her two cubs were forced out of Wisconsin by a forest fire. The bears swam across Lake Michigan toward safety in Michigan. After many hours, the mother bear reached the shore and climbed atop a bluff to watch for her cubs' arrival. Neither little bear made it. The Great Spirit Manitou created a solitary dune to mark the mother's waiting point, and the two islands, North and South Manitou, honor where the cubs were lost.

Pierce Stocking Drive

231-326-4700 • nps.gov/slbe

Pierce Stocking Drive is a paved, 7.5-mile drive into the heart of the **Sleeping Bear Dunes National Lakeshore**. Through tunnels of hardwoods (which are particularly beautiful in the fall), up, over, and around the park's ancient tree-covered dunes, the drive provides access to trailheads and several picnic areas before culminating at the spectacular **Lake Michigan Overlook**, which rises 450 feet above the surface of Lake Michigan.

Sleeping Bear, the park's primary dune, is a perched dune that sits high upon a Lake Michigan bluff. This massive dune and its neighboring sand dunes are easily admired and photographed from the overlook. The observation area also offers access to a series of footpaths and boardwalks that offer unparalleled views of Lake Michigan.

You'll see people running down the steep face of the dune toward Lake Michigan. But don't do it. It's more work than it looks to climb back up and can prove dangerous. Head to the nearby **Dune Climb** instead.

Pierce Stocking Drive (Courtesy of Traverse City Tourism)

Sleeping Bear Heritage Trail (Courtesy of Traverse City Tourism)

Sleeping Bear Heritage Trail

231-326-4700 • nps.gov/slbe

This hard-surfaced, nonmotorized, multiuse trail leads walkers, cyclists, wheelers, and skiers to most of the highlights of the **Sleeping Bear Dunes National Lakeshore**. The route stretches 22 miles (plans are to add another five miles eventually) with trailheads and parking areas approximately every 2.5 miles. The easiest way to access the trail is from the pleasant summer resort towns of Empire or Glen Arbor, in the national lakeshore's ghost town of **Glen Haven**, and at the park's **Dune Climb**. Most trailheads are furnished with restrooms, picnic areas, and drinking water.

A common strategy for making use of the Heritage Trail is to park your car and use the trail as a pleasant, environmentally friendly means of transport to and from the next park highlight. Along the path, you'll immerse yourself in the immense natural beauty of the Lake Michigan dunes, with its golden sand and thick stands of mature beech and sugar maples.

Cherry Public House

6026 S Lake St., Glen Arbor • 231-226-3033
cherryrepublic.com/cherry-public-house

✔ Cherry Republic is a landmark in Glen Arbor. The beloved store celebrates northwest Michigan's ubiquitous fruit with more than 200 cherry-themed food items and gifts. Cookies, pies, jams, honey, coffee, hot cocoa, granola, peanut butter, and barbecue sauce all include cherries.

You can find Cherry Republic stores in tourist-friendly destinations across Michigan. But here in Glen Arbor, where the business was launched, Cherry Republic's location is more of a campus, with three buildings. After shopping the Cherry Republic store, follow the meandering pathways past perennial gardens and cherry trees for a tasting at the Winery in Glen Arbor (all vintages include at least a splash of cherry juice). Then dig into lunch or dinner at the Cherry Public House. The menu includes garden salads topped with fresh veggies and cherries, cherry barbecue chicken or ribs, cherry chicken salad wraps, and cherry pie or cookies for dessert.

Cherry Public House (Courtesy of Traverse City Tourism)

Nearby Alternatives

Outdoors: South Manitou Island

The most easily accessed of Sleeping Bear's islands, South Manitou is popular for its scenic hiking trails, backpacking, and exceptionally beautiful primitive campgrounds. Once on the island, hiking trails lead to the shipwrecked ***Francisco Morazan***, with its masts poking above water, an old-growth cedar forest, a lighthouse, and pristine beaches. For day trips and overnight camping, head to Leland's famed **Fishtown** to hop on the Manitou Island Transit (manitoutransit.com).

231-326-4700
nps.gov/slbe

Discover: Glen Haven Village

Set within the park's mainland boundaries, this company town operated for more than 50 years, first as a supplier of cordwood to Great Lakes steamers, and later as a fruit cannery. Glen Haven was abandoned in 1931, but the ghost town remains. Its restored general store, boathouse, and blacksmith are open to the public.

M-109
231-326-4700
nps.gov/slbe

Activity: Dune Climb

Climbing up and running down Lake Michigan's sand dunes are perennially popular activities at **Sleeping Bear**. The broad, soft incline of the park's Dune Climb provides lots of space to explore. At the top, enjoy views of Lake Michigan and **Little Glen Lake**. A picnic area lies at the dune's base.

M-109
231-326-4700
nps.gov/slbe

Activity: Platte River Point Beach

The Platte River empties into Lake Michigan at Platte River Point, offering an opportunity to play in both bodies of water. Splash in the shallow, warm river water; swim or boogie board in the colder Lake Michigan surf; or do both. Platte River Point is a popular terminus for tubing and paddling trips on the river.

Lake Michigan Rd.
231-326-4700
nps.gov/slbe

Trip Planning

Sleeping Bear Dunes National Lakeshore

9922 Front St., Empire
231-326-4700
nps.gov/slbe

MUNISING
SENEY
SENEY NWR
HIAWATHA NATIONAL FOREST
MANISTIQUE LAKE
ENGADINE
MANISTIQUE
DAFTER
HIAWATHA NATIONAL FOREST
ST JOSEPH ISLAND
DE TOUR VILLAGE
DRUMMOND ISLAND
ST IGNACE
MACKINAC ISLAND
BOIS BLANC
MACKINAW CITY
BEAVER ISLAND
CHEBOYGAN
BURT LAKE
MULLETT LAKE
BLACK LAKE
ROGERS CITY
PETOSKEY
INDIAN RIVER
LAKE CHARLEVOIX
BOYNE FALLS
ALPENA
MANITOU ISLANDS
GAYLORD
FLETCHER POND
THUNDER BAY
TORCH LAKE
ATLANTA
HUBBARD LAKE
GLEN ARBOR
ELK RAPIDS
MANCELONA
TRAVERSE CITY
GRAYLING
MIO
HARRISVILLE
HURON NATIONAL FOREST
FRANKFORT
TAWAS CITY
BEAR LAKE
MESICK
WEST BRANCH
MANISTEE
CADILLAC
HOUGHTON LAKE
STANDISH
LUDINGTON
SAGINAW BAY
BALDWIN
SEBEWAING
MANISTEE NATIONAL FOREST
SILVER LAKE SAND DUNES
SHELBY
MARLETTE
ELK RAPIDS
TRAVERSE CITY
131
LAKE MICHIGAN
DEARBORN
SOUTH HAVEN
BENTON HARBOR
THREE RIVERS
COLDWATER
HUDSON
ADRIAN
MONROE
NILES

TRAVERSE CITY

SET ALONGSIDE THE sparkling waters of Lake Michigan's Grand Traverse Bay, surrounded by rolling hills, fruit orchards and wineries, and just a short drive from some of the state's finest golf courses and ski resorts, Traverse City has become a popular base for travelers to northern Michigan. Once known primarily for its cherries, Traverse City has increasingly developed a reputation for producing some of the state's finest wines. Take a scenic drive through Traverse City's countryside and you're as likely to see tidy rows of grapevines as acres of orchards.

Traverse City's distinct four-season climate makes this region of Michigan a favorite among outdoor enthusiasts. In spring, the Old Mission and Leelanau Peninsulas explode with colorful cherry blossoms. In summer, **Grand Traverse Bay** and the **Sleeping Bear Dunes National Lakeshore** offer great places to swim, boat, and fish. In fall, spectacular foliage forms a backdrop for the wine crush. In winter, a thick blanket of snow translates into winter sports and cozy inn stays. And back in town, Traverse City offers a thriving arts and food scene all year long.

Keith J. Charters Traverse City State Park

1132 US 31 N • 231-922-5270
michigandnr.com/parksandtrails

Lake Michigan forms a beautiful setting for life in Traverse City, whether your visit revolves around shopping and dining, wine tasting, or biking. And while you'll find several good access points to the beach, the best place to sink your toes into the sand is at Traverse City State Park, nestled at the base of the East Arm of **Grand Traverse Bay**. This state park marries the best qualities of a city park with opportunities for quiet forested camping.

Traverse City State Park's day-use area includes a quarter-mile stretch of white sugar sand. In addition to the swimming beach, there's a lakeside kiosk that rents out kayaks and SUPs, a playground, and a picnic area. A pedestrian bridge leads across busy US-31 to the park's wooded 75-acre section that includes a modern campground with spacious, shady campsites, a lodge, and mini cabins. The paved 10.5-mile TART Trail parallels the state park, providing a motor-free route into Traverse City.

Grand Traverse Bay (Courtesy of Traverse City Tourism)

Mari Vineyards, Old Mission Peninsula Wine Trail (Courtesy of Traverse City Tourism)

Old Mission Peninsula Wine Trail

M-37 • 231-947-1120
ompwinetrail.com

You'll discover at least 40 wineries in the Traverse City area, all of them producing fine, cool-weather wines: pinot grigios, Rieslings, pinot noirs, and cabernet francs. In a region once dominated by cherry orchards—northwest Michigan still produces nearly 75 percent of the nation's tart cherries—it was on the narrow Old Mission Peninsula that wine production first took root here. These days, you'll see more wine trellises than orchards on this peninsula. Follow M-37 as it twists and turns over ancient dunes, past inviting restaurants and tasting rooms, nearly all of which offer views of this spectacular landscape of vineyards and Grand Traverse Bay.

Old Mission's original winery is the award-winning **Chateau Grand Traverse**. But there are at least a dozen tasting rooms worth vising, including **Black Star Farms, Brys Estate**, and **2 Lads.** A lovely winery B&B at **Chateau Chantal** allows visitors to overnight surrounded by Michigan's loveliest wine region.

Trattoria Stella

1200 W 11th St. • 231-929-8989 • stellatc.com

The Village at Grand Traverse Commons represents one of the nation's largest historic preservation and creative reuse projects. **The Commons** was founded in the 1880s as the Northern Michigan Asylum. Elegant, brick Victorian-Italianate buildings housed patients under the "Beauty Is Therapy" philosophy. Fast-forward about 100 years, and those abandoned buildings found new life as a mixed-use, 63-acre complex housing residential units, boutique shops, a winery, brewery, coffee roastery, artisan bakery, and several restaurants and cafés.

Trattoria Stella ranks as the go-to fine dining experience at the Commons. The dining room sits below ground, its honey-colored brick interior divided into tiny nooks with linen- and crystal-laden tables, perfect for a romantic dinner out. Italian cuisine dominates the menu, which includes handcrafted cocktails of Michigan spirits, house-made pasta, and locally sourced lamb and pork. You'll find Traverse City vintages on the wine menu and can wrap up your dinner with house-baked Italian cakes and pastries.

Trattoria Stella (Courtesy of Traverse City Tourism)

Nearby Alternatives

Museum: Dennos Museum Center

Regional, national, and international art from the 19th to 21st centuries fills the galleries at the Dennos Museum, part of Northwestern Michigan College. The museum's defining collection is Inuit art of the Canadian Arctic, and ranks as one of the largest and most complete such compilations in the US.

1701 E Front St.
231-995-1055
dennosmuseum.org

Discover: M-22

In an area famous for scenic drives, Traverse City's M-22 stands out. The route leads north out of town to skirt the edges of the **Leelanau Peninsula**, a 116-mile journey past sparkling bays and boutique wineries, through charming resort towns like Glen Arbor and Leland, and beneath a tunnel of trees that explodes with color in autumn.

231-947-1120
traversecity.com

Discover: Grand Traverse Lighthouse

Set at the northernmost tip of the **Leelanau Peninsula**, the red-and-white 1858 Grand Traverse Lighthouse stands in vibrant contrast to the surrounding forest and blue waters of Lake Michigan. The lighthouse is open during warm weather months for tower climbs and a visit of the 1920s-era keeper's quarters.

15310 N Lighthouse Point Rd., Northport
231-386-5422
michigandnr.com/parksandtrails

Outdoors: TART Trail

This 10.5-mile paved, nonmotorized trail is hugely popular with cyclists, in-line skaters, walkers, and joggers. The corridor stretches across Traverse City's urban area, passing popular stops like **Traverse City State Park, Clinch Park**, and the **West End Beach**. The route joins up with an expansive network of regional bike trails, including the **Leelanau Trail**.

Bunker Hill Rd.
231-941-4300
traversetrails.org

Trip Planning

Traverse City Tourism

101 W Grandview Pkwy.
231-947-1120
traversecity.com

SUPERIOR
CANADA
MANISTEE
55
31
LUDINGTON
SAULT STE MARIE
ST JOSEPH ISLAND
DE TOUR VILLAGE
DRUMMOND ISLAND
BLACK LAKE
ROGERS CITY
INDIAN RIVER
GAYLORD
FLETCHER POND
ATLANTA
HUBBARD LAKE
MANCELONA
TRAVERSE CITY
GRAYLING
MIO
HURON NATIONAL FOREST
FRANKFORT
BEAR LAKE
MESICK
CADILLAC
HOUGHTON LAKE
WEST BRANCH
STANDISH
HARRISON
REED CITY
EVART
CLARE
WIXOM LAKE
SAGINAW BAY
BALDWIN
MANISTEE NATIONAL FOREST
MIDLAND
SILVER LAKE SAND DUNES
SHELBY
BIG RAPIDS
MT PLEASANT
BAY CITY
WHITE CLOUD
ST LOUIS
SAGINAW
HOWARD CITY
MICHIGAN
MUSKEGON
CLIO
GRAND HAVEN
OWOSSO
ST JOHNS
GRAND RAPIDS
PORTLAND
WYOMING
FENTON
LANSING
LAKE MICHIGAN

LUDINGTON

THE LAKE MICHIGAN town of Ludington owes its name to James Ludington, a 19th-century lumber baron who got rich harvesting the area's vast swaths of forest and shipping the timber via Lake Michigan. He and numerous successful lumber and shipping magnates built the grand Victorian and Italianate residences on Ludington Avenue, the city's main street, many of which have since been converted into luxurious B&Bs and inns.

Ludington is still synonymous with maritime shipping—there's a wonderful Maritime Museum that focuses on cross-lake ferries—as well as beaches and lighthouses. Ludington State Park is widely considered one of the finest in Michigan, but you can also enjoy the sand, surf, and lighthouse at Stearns Park. Many associate Ludington with the SS *Badger*, a rail, car, and passenger ferry built to transport goods to Wisconsin in the 1950s and still in service today.

Downtown, Ludington Avenue is lined with contemporary shopping, restaurants, and bars. But you only need to head east of downtown, where all those impressive B&Bs stand, or to the Port of Ludington Museum on the waterfront for reminders of the rich history of Ludington.

Ludington State Park

8800 W M-116 • 231-843-2423 • michigandnr.com/parksandtrails

The approach to Ludington State Park is among the most beautiful of any Michigan state park. M-116 passes through a portion of the park's seven-mile beach, along the way winding between wild, windswept dunes, offering glimpses of the Lake Michigan shore and multiple roadside pull-offs. The star of Ludington State Park is the iconic black-and-white-striped Big Sable Point Lighthouse, built in 1867. The light is open for tours in summer and is accessed via a pleasant 1.8-mile trail.

Inland, Ludington State Park offers access to 5,000-acre **Hamlin Lake**, its quieter and warmer water appealing when Lake Michigan's surf is too cold for swimming. Also within the park are nearly 350 wooded campsites spread between three campgrounds, 21 miles of hiking trails, and fantastic fishing. In winter, Ludington State Park is a popular snowshoeing and cross-country skiing destination. The lighthouse is particularly beautiful when surrounded by a backdrop of thick snow and ice.

Big Sable Point Lighthouse, Ludington State Park
(Courtesy of Amy S. Eckert)

Port of Ludington Maritime Museum (Courtesy of Kim Skeltis for Pure Ludington)

✓ Port of Ludington Maritime Museum

217 S Lakeshore Dr. • 231-843-4808 • ludingtonmaritimemuseum.org

Ludington's car ferry history forms the centerpiece of this interactive museum. The three-story museum is located in a historic coast guard boathouse, on the very channel where the car ferry SS *Badger* and a century of her predecessors have long sailed. Life aboard these ferries and other Great Lakes vessels is laid out in fascinating detail through artifacts, photos, and interactive displays. No exhibit better reveals the difficulty of maneuvering such a massive ship as the virtual game that challenges visitors to pilot the *Pere Marquette* into **Ludington Harbor.** It's more difficult than it looks!

Other exhibits worth viewing include lighthouse evolution and the groundbreaking development of the Fresnel lens; a lineup of more than 150 lighthouse models; the shipwrecks along the Lake Michigan shore, known as the **Sunset Coast**; and the story of the devastating Armistice Day Storm of 1940, which killed more than 150 civilians and sailors in Ludington.

House of Flavors

402 W Ludington Ave. • 231-845-5785 • houseofflavorsrestaurants.com

The House of Flavors is a landmark in downtown Ludington. Launched in 1948 as **Park Dairy**, an operation that produced milk, butter, cottage cheese, and five flavors of ice cream, the business turned its focus strictly to ice cream in 1959 and changed its name to House of Flavors in 1964. House of Flavors expanded to become a full-service restaurant and ice cream parlor in 1976, and today produces more than 30 million gallons of ice cream per year.

Although you can also order breakfast until well into the afternoon, sandwiches and wraps, burgers, hot dogs, and salads make up the majority of House of Flavors' menu—perfect fare for beach days. But ice cream remains House of Flavors's hot seller, so to speak. In summer, expect to see a long lineup of customers waiting for heaping helpings of nearly 40 flavors, plus sundaes, shakes, sorbets, and frozen yogurt. It's worth the wait.

House of Flavors (Courtesy of Tom and Brad Reed Photography)

Nearby Alternatives

Museum: Sandcastles Children's Museum

One of Michigan's best children's museums, Sandcastles is the perfect stop when you need a break from the beach. Kids can climb into the vintage 1958 Cessna four-seater that hangs in the museum lobby, fill kid-size carts with kid-size grocery food, dig sand in the construction zone, and test their strength on an indoor climbing wall.

129 E Ludington Ave.
231-233-9326
sandcastleschildrensmuseum.com

Activity: Waterfront Park

Waterfront Park encompasses five acres of broad green lawns and colorful flower gardens packed with activities. Check out the bronze Ludington-themed sculptures, enjoy the playground, catch an evening sunset, and get comfortable at the bandshell where evening concerts regularly take place. The park sits between two marinas and offers a great observation point for SS *Badger* sailings.

W Filer St. between S William and S Robert Streets
231-845-6237
ludington.mi.us

Museum: Historic White Pine Village

Ludington's living history museum offers a glimpse of life in the area in the 19th and early 20th centuries. Thirty historic buildings and vehicles include a courthouse, a sawmill, residences, a locomotive, and a flat car piled with a load of West Michigan lumber. Artifacts further detail life from more than a century ago.

1687 S Lakeshore Dr.
231-843-4808
historicwhitepinevillage.org

Restaurant: Crown and Cork

This waterfront kitchen and bar offers an upscale dining option in downtown Ludington. With a view of Ludington's harbor front, the restaurant offers a casual menu of salads, sandwiches, and burgers, as well as choice steaks, local whitefish, and salmon alongside locally sourced produce and craft cocktails.

502 W Loomis St.
231-425-3557
crownncork.com

Trip Planning:

Ludington Area Convention & Visitors Bureau

119 S Rath Ave.
800-542-4600
pureludington.com

SILVER LAKE SAND DUNES
SHELBY
MANISTEE NATIONAL FOREST
31
GRAND ISLAND
GRAND MARAIS
TAHQUAMENON FALLS STATE PARK
SAULT STE MARIE
MUNISING
SENEY
DAFTER
ST JOSEPH ISLAND
TRENARY
HIAWATHA NATIONAL FOREST
DE TOUR VILLAGE
DRUMMOND ISLAND
ALPENA
THUNDER BAY
FLETCHER POND
ATLANTA
HUBBARD LAKE
HARRISVILLE
MIO
HURON NATIONAL FOREST
TAWAS CITY
WEST BRANCH
HOUGHTON LAKE
CADILLAC
MANISTEE
STANDISH
HARRISON
LUDINGTON
REED CITY
EVART
CLARE
WIXOM LAKE
SAGINAW BAY
BALDWIN
MIDLAND
BIG RAPIDS
MT PLEASANT
BAY CITY
WHITE CLOUD
ST LOUIS
SAGINAW
HOWARD CITY
MICHIGAN
MUSKEGON
CLIO
GRAND HAVEN
GRAND RAPIDS
ST JOHNS
OWOSSO
FLINT
LAKE MICHIGAN
WYOMING
PORTLAND
FENTON
OXFORD
HOLLAND
LANSING
SAUGATUCK
HASTINGS
BRIGHTON
CHARLOTTE
ALLEGAN
ANN ARBOR
SOUTH HAVEN
BATTLE CREEK
JACKSON

SILVER LAKE SAND DUNES

THE SILVER LAKE Sand Dunes form an imposing golden barrier between Lake Michigan and Silver Lake. Blowing slowly westward in the Great Lakes breeze, the dunes span some 2,000 acres of the state park. Finding ways to experience and play in the dunes and their adjacent lakes is what most visitors to the area focus on.

There is more to the Silver Lake area than sand dunes. The region incorporates three towns: Mears, Hart, and Silver Lake. Within these small communities you'll find locally grown produce (the area is famous for its fruit and asparagus), fresh-baked pies, and jams for sale at farm markets and small roadside stands. **Lewis Adventure Farm and Zoo** combines a farm market with a playground and farm-themed activities, including a petting zoo and displays of such exotic animals as lemurs, capybaras, and sloths. And the nearby towns of **Pentwater** and **Ludington** make good day trips for boutique shopping, dining, and a children's museum.

But if it's sand dunes you're looking for, Silver Lake offers plenty of opportunities to enjoy them, in every season.

Silver Lake State Park

9679 W State Park Rd. • 231-873-3083 • michigandnr.com/parksandtrails

✓ Three miles of Lake Michigan shoreline and 2,000 acres of dunes mark the high points of Silver Lake State Park. The golden dunes and their two lakes—powerful Lake Michigan and calmer, warmer Silver Lake—offer good options for the boaters, anglers, and swimmers who spend their summers at this vacation hot spot.

A 500-acre section of Silver Lake State Park offers the only dunes east of the Mississippi River open to ORVs, and it's a wildly popular destination in summer. To protect the landscape from overuse, entry and permitting requirements apply to those bringing their own vehicles. Dune buggy, boat, and bicycle rentals are available locally.

A segment of the **Silver Lake Sand Dunes** is always reserved for pedestrians. Wandering the impressive natural landscape is a powerful experience. Silver Lake State Park also includes a popular modern campground and the elegant Little Sable Point Lighthouse.

Little Sable Point Lighthouse, Silver Lake State Park
(Courtesy of Silver Lake Sand Dunes-Hart Visitors Bureau)

Mac Wood's Dune Rides (Courtesy of Silver Lake Sand Dunes-Hart Visitors Bureau)

Mac Wood's Dune Rides

629 N 18th Ave., Mears • 231-873-2817 • macwoodsdunerides.com

☑ Mac Wood's was founded in 1930, when the owners first strapped visitors into souped-up dune buggies and whisked them up and over Silver Lake's massive dune field. Nearly a century later, visitors still clamor for an opportunity to join these guided tours of West Michigan's most famous landmark. The iconic red dune buggies can accommodate up to 25 guests who head out for a 40-minute ride through seven miles of sand dunes, powering up steep slopes, whipping around hairpin turns. Along the way, the driver shares information about the history, geology, flora, and fauna of this unique landscape, interspersed with a few corny jokes. The tour includes quick photo stops along a soaring ridge, with jaw-dropping views of the dunes and their lakes, and at the Lake Michigan shore.

Concern about the erosion of the dunes has strictly limited access by commercial operators. Mac Wood's remains the only commercial tour company permitted within the natural area.

Big Hart Brewing Co.

4086 W Polk Rd., Hart • 231-301-8226 • bighartbrewing.com

☑ Big Hart Brewing and its logo play off the name of the community they're located in, Hart. But the staff behind the brewery truly have a heart for Oceana County and the Silver Lake area and are committed to using locally sourced ingredients to showcase their home turf.

The brewery's taproom and dining room sit in a large building about eight miles east of **Silver Lake State Park**. Hard ciders and stouts, session beers, alt beers, British- and German-style—the beer lineup at Big Hart is broad and varies with the season. House-distilled spirits include gin, vodka, and whiskey, and you can also order a glass of house wine if you prefer. The food menu includes the good, hearty fare you expect in a resort community focused on outdoor recreation: burgers, wings, generously sized sandwiches, salads topped with locally grown produce, and a kids' menu.

Big Hart Brewing Co.
(Courtesy of Amy S. Eckert)

Nearby Alternatives

Activity: Craig's Cruisers
This beloved family amusement park offers lots of fun when you need a break from the beach. Enjoy a small roller coaster, go-carts, bumper cars, paddleboats, a zip line, mini golf, and a large arcade a short bike ride away from Silver Lake State Park.
8343 W Hazel Rd., Mears
231-873-2511
craigscruisers.com

Restaurant: Silver Scoops
You can order barbecue, sandwiches, and hot dogs at Silver Scoops, but this downtown favorite specializes in ice cream. Order from 20 different flavors of scooped hard, soft serve, and nondairy ice creams, shakes, and flurries. The restaurant is take-out only but offers lots of shaded picnic tables outside.
8450 W Hazel Rd., Mears
231-742-8178
silverlakesilverscoops.com

Outdoors: Hart-Montague Trail State Park This popular converted rail trail leads 22 miles through rural landscapes, beneath mature hardwoods, and alongside small towns and picnic areas. The multiuse path is paved and well-marked, a good choice for even the youngest riders. Find a large parking area and trailhead on W Polk Road between US-31 and South State Street in Hart.
231-869-2051
michigandnr.com/parksandtrails

Shopping and Dining: Pentwater
This walkable resort community 15 miles from Silver Lake offers an upscale shopping and dining alternative. Pick up resort wear and art at the boutique shops or enjoy a meal out. Favorites include the **Cottage Garden Café**, with its beautiful screen porch; the **Village Café** with steak, seafood, and cocktails; and **Green Isaac's Coffee & Tea.**
324 S Hancock St.
231-869-4150
pentwater.org

Trip Planning

Silver Lake Visitors Bureau
2388 N Comfort Dr., Hart
231-873-2247
thinkdunes.com

61
WIXOM
LAKE
10
MIDLAND
GRAND MARAIS
TAHQUAMENON FALLS
SAULT STE MARIE
MUNISING
SENEY
SENEY NWR
MANITOULIN ISLANDS
THUNDER BAY
LAKE HURON
HARRISVILLE
HURON NATIONAL FOREST
TAWAS CITY
FRANKFORT
BEAR LAKE
MESICK
MANISTEE
CADILLAC
HOUGHTON LAKE
WEST BRANCH
STANDISH
HARRISON
LUDINGTON
REED CITY
EVART
CLARE
SAGINAW BAY
HARBOR BEACH
SEBEWAING
BALDWIN
MANISTEE NATIONAL FOREST
BIG RAPIDS
MT PLEASANT
BAY CITY
SILVER LAKE SAND DUNES
SHELBY
WHITE CLOUD
ST LOUIS
SAGINAW
SANDUSKY
MARLETTE
HOWARD CITY
MICHIGAN
MUSKEGON
CLIO
LAPEER
GRAND HAVEN
GRAND RAPIDS
ST JOHNS
OWOSSO
FLINT
FRANKENMUTH
OXFORD
WYOMING
PORTLAND
FENTON
PONTIAC
HOLLAND
LANSING
SAUGATUCK
HASTINGS
BRIGHTON
CHARLOTTE
DETROIT
ALLEGAN
ANN ARBOR
DEARBORN
SOUTH HAVEN
BATTLE CREEK
KALAMAZOO
JACKSON

MIDLAND

MIDLAND SITS AT the crook of Michigan's Thumb, near the base of Lake Huron's sparkling Saginaw Bay. Originally a city of loggers and lumbermen, Midland grew in prominence and wealth thanks to the arrival of Herbert Henry Dow, who arrived in 1890 and established the Dow Chemical Company. Now the home of Dow Chemical and Dow Corning, Midland continues to be a center of industrial and energy innovation.

Herbert's son Alden B. Dow further pushed Midland into the limelight as a progressive architect of the Midwestern modern style. The younger Dow designed dozens of buildings, many of which were located in his hometown of Midland.

Midland enjoys a wealth of natural beauty, owing partly to its location at the Tittabawassee and Chippewa Rivers and Lake Huron. But the Dows can be credited for the creation of the **Dow Gardens**, formerly the family estate, and its adjacent forest. More than 400 **midcentury modern architectural sites** lie within the city limits as well, providing Midland with a sense of style and design uncommon in most cities of its size.

Dow Gardens

1809 Eastman Ave. • 800-362-4874 • dowgardens.org

✓ The 110 beautifully landscaped acres of the Dow Gardens trace their roots to Herbert Dow, the founder of **Dow Chemical**, and his wife Grace. The couple purchased the property in 1899 and slowly transformed it with the addition of annual and perennial display beds, ornamental trees, streams and fountains, and gracefully arching bridges. The gardens' conservatory was designed by Herbert and Grace's son Alden, the midcentury modern architectural talent, in 1975. It was renovated and expanded in 2023 and includes a popular butterfly house each spring. **The Pines**, the house where the Dows raised their seven children, remains a popular stop on a tour of the Dow Gardens.

Dow Gardens (Courtesy of Great Lakes Bay Regional CVB)

Alden B. Dow Home and Studio (Courtesy of Great Lakes Bay Regional CVB)

Alden B. Dow Home & Studio

315 Post St. • 989-839-2744 • abdow.org

✓ The midcentury modern masterpiece that was architect Alden B. Dow's home and studio ranks as one of the highlights of a visit to Midland. After having studied under Frank Lloyd Wright, Alden designed his own home in Midland, completing it in 1941. An extravaganza of copper and glass, specialty cinder blocks and organically designed furniture, geometric shapes, and natural motifs, the home seems to grow out of and flow into the landscape and incorporates natural light and sprawling vistas. Expect a cornucopia of human artistry and an homage to the very ground that the home sits on. "Gardens never end and buildings never begin" was Alden's mantra.

Guided tours offer visitors an opportunity to explore the 20,000-square-foot home, with docents sharing along the way the design philosophy that guided Alden B. Dow's plans. Consider the multiday architecture and design camps for children or adults. Activities range from canoeing Alden's glassy lake to engaging in hands-on design workshops.

Café Zinc

111 W Main St. • 989-839-0500 • thehhotel.com

✔ Set within Midland's finest lodging, the H Hotel, Café Zinc serves breakfast, lunch, and dinner within an easy walk of downtown Midland and the pleasant walking paths near the Tittabawassee and Chippewa Rivers. There's also a beautiful patio on Main Street, a great spot for people watching in warm weather months.

Café Zinc's logo is the chemical symbol for zinc, Zn. This is Midland, after all, home of Dow Chemical. Inside, the restaurant's decor is inspired by European bistro dining: crisp white walls and table linens, a lovely tile floor in geometric designs. But where the traditional Parisian bistro features zinc countertops, Midland's Zinc Café features an eye-catching platinum ceiling.

Café Zinc's menu takes inspiration from the French bistro tradition, too. Omelets, quiches, and benedicts are the rule at breakfast time. Lunch and dinner incorporate soups and creative salads, Mediterranean wraps and Croques Monsieur, tartines, grilled fish, and steak frites.

Café Zinc (Courtesy of Great Lakes Bay Regional CVB)

Nearby Alternatives

Outdoors: Canopy Walk

Measuring 1,400 feet, the nation's longest canopy walk escorts visitors 40 feet high for a bird's-eye view of the surrounding **Whiting Forest**. The accessible walkway incorporates three viewing platforms, rope cargo nets, and seed-shaped climbing pods, accommodating those who want to play in the treetops and those who merely want to admire them.

Eastman Ave.
800-362-4874
dowgardens.org/forest

Outdoors: Chippewa Nature Center

Nineteen miles of trails meander through this natural area on the Chippewa and Pine Rivers. Visit in spring and summer to admire the center's wildflowers and in autumn to take in the brilliant fall foliage. The park also includes a historic farmstead and schoolhouse, a maple sugarhouse, and a nature center with a nice ecosystem gallery.

400 S Badour Rd.
989-631-0830
chippewanaturecenter.org

Discover: Midcentury Modern Midland

If seeing Alden B. Dow's exceptionally crafted midcentury masterpiece isn't enough to satisfy you, set out on a trek to discover the rest of Midland's architectural gems. Fifty midcentury architects and architectural firms left their mark on this city. Download the mobile app for a self-guided tour.

midcenturymidland.org

Outdoors: Pere Marquette Rail Trail

Thirty miles of paved, flat trail lead from Midland to the town of Clare, a multiuse corridor popular with runners, cyclists, in-line skaters, and strollers. The trail meanders through beautiful hardwood forest and parallels the Tittabawassee River, passing through downtown Midland. The trail connects to the **Chippewa and Pere Marquette State Trails**.

415 W Irish St.
989-687-2396
peremarquetterailtrail.org

Trip Planning

Go Great Lakes Bay/Midland Travel

128 E Main St.
800-444-9979
gogreat.com/cities/midland

SENEY
SENEY NWR
MANISTIQUE LAKE
ENGADINE
MANISTIQUE
HIAWATHA NATIONAL FOREST
DAFTER
ST JOSEPH ISLAND
DE TOUR VILLAGE
DRUMMOND ISLAND
ST IGNACE
MACKINAC ISLAND
MANITOULIN ISLANDS
BEAVER ISLAND
LAPEER
FRANKENMUTH
OXFORD
53
MANITOU ISLANDS
LAKE HURON
BEAR LAKE
LUDINGTON
BALDWIN
MANISTEE NATIONAL FOREST
SHELBY
WHITE CLOUD
BIG RAPIDS
MT PLEASANT
BAY CITY
SAGINAW
ST LOUIS
HARBOR BEACH
SANDUSKY
MARLETTE
HOWARD CITY
MICHIGAN
MUSKEGON
CLIO
LAPEER
PORT HURON
GRAND HAVEN
GRAND RAPIDS
ST JOHNS
OWOSSO
FRANKENMUTH
OXFORD
PORTLAND
FENTON
WYOMING
HOLLAND
LANSING
PONTIAC
SAUGATUCK
HASTINGS
BRIGHTON
CHARLOTTE
ALLEGAN
DETROIT
LAKE ST CLAIR
ANN ARBOR
DEARBORN
SOUTH HAVEN
BATTLE CREEK
KALAMAZOO
JACKSON
CANADA
BENTON HARBOR
JONESVILLE
THREE RIVERS
COLDWATER
ADRIAN
MONROE
HUDSON
NILES

FRANKENMUTH

THE CHARMING TOWN of Frankenmuth was settled in 1845 by German missionaries to eastern Michigan. Locals still honor that heritage, giving the town the moniker "Little Bavaria." Bavarian-inspired architecture, menus, shops, festivals, and street and business names recall the town's beginnings and make for a pleasant and memorable getaway.

Much of the Bavarian-themed activity in Frankenmuth centers around the Bavarian Inn and Zehnder's. Both hospitality businesses offer German-inspired restaurants, lodging, indoor water parks for the family, and German-themed shops. Both businesses also happen to trace their roots to the same Zehnder ancestors. Besides these businesses, you'll find a downtown with similar Bavarian-themed architecture, shopping, and dining, a traditional wooden bridge (the *Holz Brücke*), and the Frankenmuth Brewery (Michigan's oldest).

Frankenmuth is also known for its festivals, many of them German themed. Time your visit to join the Bavarian Festival, Zehnder's Snow Fest, and, naturally, a rousing Oktoberfest. The annual Frankenmuth Dog Bowl, the world's largest Olympic-style festival for dogs, does not have German roots, but it's a lot of fun nonetheless.

Bavarian Inn Glockenspiel

713 S Main St. • 989-652-9941 • bavarianinn.com

Frankenmuth's Glockenspiel Tower adorns the facade of the Bavarian Inn and never fails to draw crowds when it chimes. The glockenspiel's 35-bell carillon, its figurine movement, which depicts the fairy tale of the Pied Piper of Hamelin, and its illuminated clock were all imported from Germany in October 1967. The clockworks and carillon are housed within a 50-foot tower. On each hour and quarter hour, the clock sounds its five-bell Westminster chime. At noon, 3:00 p.m., 6:00 p.m., and 9:00 p.m. the glockenspiel follows the clock's chime with carillon songs and the Pied Piper's performance.

Although the glockenspiel is attached to the Bavarian Inn, its daily performance can be enjoyed by the public. You might head inside anyway, for a meal of German and American specialties at **Oma's Restaurant** or the **Lorelei Lounge** or shopping for baked goods, toys, or souvenirs at the **Castle Shops**.

Bavarian Inn Glockenspiel Tower (Courtesy of Great Lakes Bay Regional CVB)

Bronner's Christmas Wonderland (Courtesy of Great Lakes Bay Regional CVB)

Bronner's Christmas Wonderland

25 Christmas Ln. • 989-652-9931
bronners.com

☑ Wally Bronner began his career in the Christmas decor business in 1945 after designing holiday lamppost decorations for a nearby community. Less than a decade later, Bronner's Christmas shop was a brick-and-mortar operation. Decades of growth and a series of expansions finally led to the establishment of today's Bronner's Christmas Wonderland. The sprawling Christmas store ranks as the world's largest, covering nearly seven and a half acres, or the size of five and a half football fields.

More than 50,000 Christmas items are sold in the store, ranging from Christmas trees and trims to lights, wreaths, nativity scenes, nutcrackers, personalized ornaments, candles, stockings, outdoor displays, and the storage boxes for stowing it all away when the holidays are over. You can even purchase Santa suits, as John Wayne is reported to have done in 1976. More than two million guests visit Bronner's each year, making the store among the most popular tourist attractions in Frankenmuth.

Zehnder's of Frankenmuth

730 S Main St. • 844-207-7309 • zehnders.com

In a town like Frankenmuth, German food and drinks find their way onto nearly every restaurant menu. Zehnder's stands apart for its longevity, its size, and its reliably good food. The restaurant began as the Exchange Hotel in 1856, serving heaping platters of fried chicken, mashed potatoes, dressing, egg noodles, and vegetables family style. A redesign in the 1920s gave the restaurant a Mount Vernon–style facade. A neon sign (still operational and thought to be one of the nation's oldest) in 1936 added pizzazz. Still another redesign in the '50s emphasized the restaurant's German roots.

More than 150 years later, Zehnder's still serves chicken dinners family style. A single price buys all-you-can-eat salads, breads, and that original chicken menu. Order à la carte and choose from steaks, schnitzel, sausages, perch, and a handful of vegetarian offerings. The restaurant is hugely popular, and very large. The dining room can accommodate up to 1,500 people.

Nearby Alternatives

Activity: Zehnder's Splash Village Hotel and Waterpark

Frankenmuth's largest water park hotel (the **Bavarian Inn Lodge** features a very nice but smaller water park) features a rare retractable roof, allowing visitors to enjoy the sunshine in the summer months. More than 50,000 square feet of fun includes a six-story family raft ride, four-story tube slides, a lazy river, squirty toys, and a dumping bucket.

1365 S Main St.
844-330-1715
zehnders.com/zehnders-splash-village

Venue: Silent Night Memorial Chapel

The familiar Christmas carol "Silent Night" was first composed and sung in the tiny Alpine *Stille Nacht Kapelle* in Oberndorf, Austria, in 1818. Nearly 175 years later, in 1992, **Bronner's Christmas Wonderland** constructed an authorized replica of the charming little chapel on its grounds, open to the public and free of charge.

25 Christmas Ln.
989-652-9931
bronners.com

Discover: *Holz Brücke* (Wooden Bridge)

Completed in 1980, Frankenmuth's Covered Bridge spans the Cass River and ranks as Michigan's largest and the youngest two-lane, two-sidewalk wooden bridge in the world. The imposing 239-foot, 230-ton bridge is built entirely of wood and connects businesses like the **Bavarian Inn Lodge** with downtown Frankenmuth

Covered Bridge Ln.

Restaurant and Brewery: Frankenmuth Brewery

Since 1862, Frankenmuth Brewery has produced German-style ales and lagers, making it Michigan's oldest brewery. The restaurant pairs its beverages with soft pretzels and bratwurst, as you might expect. But the menu revolves around hearty sandwiches, burgers, and pizza. When the weather warms up, enjoy your food and drink on the patio, overlooking the Cass River.

425 S Main St.
989-262-8300
frankenmuthbrewery.com

Trip Planning

Frankenmuth Convention & Visitors Bureau

635 S Main St. • 800-386-8696
frankenmuth.org

MUSKEGON
GRAND HAVEN
96
37
LAKE MICHIGAN
MICHIGAN
GRAND RAPIDS
HOLLAND
LANSING
SAGINAW
MARQUETTE
GRAND MARAIS
MUNISING
SENEY
HIAWATHA NATIONAL FOREST
MANISTEE NATIONAL FOREST
HURON NATIONAL FOREST
LUDINGTON
CHEBOYGAN
MACKINAC ISLAND
ESCANABA
HOUGHTON LAKE

MUSKEGON

THE CITY OF Muskegon credits much of its early growth to the success of the lumber industry. In the 19th century, more than 50 sawmills were based in the Muskegon area, which in turn produced more than 40 millionaires.

The wealth that Muskegon's lumber heritage accumulated can be seen in some spectacular cultural institutions. Begin with the opulent Victorian **Hackley and Hume Houses**, the personal residences of Muskegon's preeminent lumber barons. Then head off to the Muskegon Art Museum, which benefitted from the philanthropy of Charles Hackley and was funded in large part by a bequest from the magnate.

The very Lake Michigan waterways that facilitated industrial development in the 19th and 20th centuries make Muskegon a terrific Great Lakes getaway today. Muskegon is home to three state parks: **Muskegon, P. J. Hoffmaster, and Duck Lake**. Combined, these natural areas protect wide swaths of golden sand dunes and mixed forest, and include 5.5 miles of Lake Michigan shoreline, two inland lakes, three campgrounds, a dozen miles of hiking and cross-country skiing trails, picnic areas, and playgrounds.

Muskegon State Park

3560 Memorial Dr. • 231-744-3480 • michigandnr.com/parksandtrails

The **Muskegon Luge Adventure Sports Park** forms a unique addition to the golden beaches, sand dunes, cherry-red lighthouse, and hiking trails of Muskegon State Park. The park's 850-foot luge track was designed by a local, three-time Olympian in the sport and is one of only four in the US. Expect a mighty adrenaline rush on this sheer ice track, with its steep descents, banks, and tight curves. After an introductory lesson, even first-timers can near speeds of 30 mph. Other attractions at the adventure park include a forested ice-skating trail, an ice hockey rink, and about 10 miles of Nordic ski and snowshoeing trails, some of which are lit after dark.

Also unique at Muskegon State Park is the **Block House**. Reminiscent of a military watchtower, the Block House was actually constructed in the 1930s by the **Civilian Conservation Corps** to provide visitors an observation deck.

Muskegon Lighthouse, Muskegon State Park
(Courtesy of Visit Muskegon)

Michigan's Adventure (Courtesy of Visit Muskegon)

Michigan's Adventure and WildWater Adventure Park

1198 W Riley-Thompson Rd. • 231-766-9959 • miadventure.com

More than 60 thrill rides, including seven roller coasters, keep families entertained at Michigan's Adventure, the largest theme park in the state. Younger children gravitate toward Camp Snoopy, with a carousel, Kiddie Cars, and Woodstock, an introductory-level roller coaster. From there, the thrills increase exponentially to include a Corkscrew, Shivering Timbers wood frame, and Thunderhawk steel roller coasters as well as rides such as the Scrambler, Rip Cord, Sea Dragon, and Flying Trapeze to thoroughly spin, swing, and bounce guests.

In summertime, Michigan's Adventure offers another avenue of fun with WildWater Adventure. Like Michigan's Adventure, the adjacent water fun park includes calmer attractions such as Boogie Beach for the youngest visitors, and more exhilarating rides like the Commotion Ocean wave pool, HydroBlaster, and the Funnel of Fear waterslide for older kids and adults. Admission to Michigan's Adventure includes entry to WildWater Adventure in season.

Lake House Waterfront Grille

730 Terrace Point Rd. • 231-722-4461 • thelakehousemi.com

When summer comes to West Michigan, everyone heads to the water. Muskegon's Lake House Waterfront Grille sits alongside the Terrace Point Marina overlooking a harbor full of elegant sailboats and cruisers. A spacious deck with pristine white table linens and wicker chairs is always popular in summer, allowing diners to soak up the sunshine and the water views outdoors. Once the boats are stored away for the season, the dining room enjoys views of the icy harbor and Muskegon Lake covered in a thick blanket of snow. A fireplace adds warmth and ambience to a winter visit to the Lake House.

Seafood makes up a significant portion of the Lake House's menu. Order pan-seared Great Lakes walleye or a lake perch sandwich, or venture to more exotic waters with a meal of scallops, salmon, crab cakes, or mussels. Non-seafood options include burgers, fine steaks, and entrée-size salads.

Lake House Waterfront Grille (Courtesy of Visit Muskegon)

Nearby Alternatives

Tour: Hackley and Hume Historic Site

When lumber barons Charles Hackley and Thomas Hume made it big in the late 1800s, they built fabulous homes to display their wealth. Visitors can walk through their spectacular examples of Victorian architecture at this historic site, each adorned with the finest finished woods, stained glass, ceramic tiles, and customized plasterwork.

484 W Webster Ave.
231-722-7578
lakeshoremuseum.org/hackley-hume

Discover: Scolnik House of the Depression Era

Period carpet, wallpaper, furniture, and other items of daily living convey the life of a West Michigan family as they faced the privations of the Great Depression. Visitors can try on clothing, listen to the radio, and explore the Victory Garden at the Scolnik's 1930s family home.

504 W. Clay Ave.
231-722-7578
lakeshoremuseum.org/scolnik-house

Museum: USS *Silversides* Submarine Museum

Tour Muskegon's authentic World War II-era submarine and get a taste of shipboard life. A visit to the *Silversides* includes a walk through the US Coast Guard Cutter *McLane* and a two-story World War II museum. Groups can book overnight stays at the *Silversides*, a rare opportunity to sleep in the berths once occupied by World War II sailors.

1346 Bluff St. • 231-755-1230
silversidesmuseum.org

Museum: Muskegon Museum of Art

An extraordinary array of American and European paintings, sculptures, prints, and drawings makes up the permanent collection of this museum, which was jump-started by lumber magnate Charles Hackley's investment. Look for works by Elizabeth Catlett, Edward Hopper, Winslow Homer, Dale Chihuly, Whistler, Pissarro, and John Steuart Curry.

296 W Webster Ave.
231-720-2570
muskegonartmuseum.org

Trip Planning

Muskegon County Convention & Visitors Bureau

610 W Western Ave.
231-724-3100
visitmuskegon.org

GRAND MARAIS
TAHQUAMENON FALLS STATE PARK
SAULT STE MARIE
SAULT STE MARIE
DAFTER
SENEY
HIAWATHA NATIONAL FOREST
MANISTIQUE LAKE
ENGADINE
ST JOSEPH ISLAND
DE TOUR VILLAGE
DRUMMOND ISLAND
ST IGNACE
MACKINAC ISLAND
BOIS BLANC
MACKINAW CITY
BEAVER ISLAND
CHEBOYGAN
MANITOULIN ISLANDS
LAKE HURON
PORT HURON
69
94
GLEN ARBOR
BEAR LAKE
BALDWIN
MANISTEE NATIONAL FOREST
BIG RAPIDS
WHITE CLOUD
HOWARD CITY
SEBEWAING
BAY CITY
SAGINAW
ST LOUIS
SANDUSKY
MARLETTE
MICHIGAN
MUSKEGON
CLIO
LAPEER
PORT HURON
GRAND HAVEN
GRAND RAPIDS
ST JOHNS
OWOSSO
FLINT
FRANKENMUTH
OXFORD
WYOMING
PORTLAND
FENTON
HOLLAND
LANSING
PONTIAC
SAUGATUCK
HASTINGS
BRIGHTON
CHARLOTTE
DETROIT
LAKE ST CLAIR
ALLEGAN
ANN ARBOR
DEARBORN
SOUTH HAVEN
BATTLE CREEK
JACKSON
CANADA
KALAMAZOO

PORT HURON

PORT HURON SITS at the base of **Michigan's Thumb**, at the southernmost point of Lake Huron and at the mouth of the St. Clair River. Through this waterway, freighters from Lakes Superior, Michigan, and Huron must pass to reach the St. Lawrence Seaway and, eventually, the Atlantic Ocean.

Life has long revolved around Great Lakes shipping in Port Huron, and watching the lumbering 1,000-foot ships passing by just a few feet from the city's riverside walkways, parks, restaurants, and hotels is a perennial pastime. Port Huron is home to two lighthouses, which are also fun to visit and photograph. But the city is not only a gateway to the Atlantic. It is also a gateway to Canada, one of three Michigan cities that allow visitors easily to visit America's northern neighbor.

Port Huron also serves as a gateway of sorts to Detroit in the south and rural northern Michigan. The city makes a good stopping point on a multiday trip. Once you're here, you'll discover enough to see and do that you may want to stay.

Lighthouse Beach Park

2900 Conger St. • 810-984-9760 • porthuronrec.com/beach

Port Huron's Fort Gratiot Light sits within Lighthouse Beach Park, where Lake Huron funnels into the St. Clair River. The light was constructed in 1829 to replace its predecessor, which collapsed after only four years of service. The existing light was clearly an improvement, as it ranks as the oldest surviving lighthouse in the Great Lakes. The light's 86-foot-tall white brick tower serves as the subject of many vacation photos, but views over Lake Huron from atop its 94 iron stairs are simply breathtaking. Tours are conducted by the Port Huron Museum and include a look at the restored keeper's quarters.

Lighthouse Beach also features a beach, naturally. This Lake Huron strand is a great family destination, easily combined with a lighthouse visit for an afternoon of beachcombing, swimming, and a picnic. There is also a playground, restrooms, and a bike station with an air pump and tools.

Fort Gratiot Lighthouse, Lighthouse Beach Park
(Courtesy of bluewater.org)

Statue of Young Thomas Edison and the Blue Water Bridge, Thomas Edison Depot Museum (Courtesy of Amy S. Eckert)

Thomas Edison Depot Museum

510 Thomas Edison Pkwy. • 810-982-0891
phmuseum.org/thomas-edison-depot-museum

☑ America's most prolific inventor is famous for having had laboratories in New Jersey and Florida, but Thomas Edison spent his school-age years in Port Huron. In his early teens, Edison worked as a newshawk, selling newspapers, candy, and cigars aboard the Grand Trunk Railway that ran from Port Huron to Detroit and back. The 1858 **Fort Gratiot Depot** building out of which Edison worked has been restored and transformed into Port Huron's Thomas Edison Depot Museum. The interactive museum recounts Edison's early family life, his struggles, his insatiable curiosity, and ultimately, his extraordinary success as an inventor and a businessman. The museum also features a few of Edison's most famous inventions, including a phonograph player and the world's largest light bulb.

Outside the museum building stands a railroad baggage car that houses a re-creation of Edison's mobile chemistry lab. A statue of young Thomas stands along the waterfront, within view of the museum.

Freighters Eatery & Taproom

800 Harker St. • 810-941-6010 • freightersph.com

☑ Crisp, fresh salads, Great Lakes whitefish, and Michigan craft-beer-battered fish, as well as many of the other ingredients on Freighters' menu, are locally sourced in a philosophy that the staff like to call "Commit to the Mitt." You can also choose from burgers, handhelds, steaks, and hearty mac 'n' cheese dishes at Freighters.

But for many, Freighters' location is the best reason to eat here. The restaurant sits at the base of the **Blue Water Bridge** to Ontario, a graceful blue span over the St. Clair River. Oversize plate-glass windows reveal the bridge in all its beauty, as well as the boats that ply the river's waters, most significantly, Great Lakes freighters. In summer, dine on the restaurant's patio beneath colorful sun umbrellas to take in the passing ships. The restaurant is connected to the **DoubleTree by Hilton Hotel** and the Blue Water Convention Center.

Freighters (Courtesy of bluewater.org)

Nearby Alternatives

Discover: Blue Water Bridge

Dating from 1938, the Blue Water Bridge forms an important international crossing between Port Huron and Sarnia, Ontario. View the soaring arch, constructed at a height sufficient to allow for passing ships, from the **Thomas Edison Parkway**, where you can also spot the **Blue Water Maiden** statue that welcomes waterborne traffic to Port Huron.

I-69/I-94 and Hwy. 402
810-985-9541
michigan.gov

Outdoors: Bridge to Bay Trail

This 50-mile multiuse trail follows the Lake Huron, Lake Saint Clair, and Saint Clair Riverbanks from Lakeport State Park to New Baltimore, passing through Port Huron along the way. The route is a mix of boardwalks, rail trails, and city bike paths that combine to form a popular excursion along the edge of Michigan's Thumb.

Thomas Edison Pkwy.
bridgetobay.org

Discover: Huron Light Ship

Constructed in 1920 as a rare floating beacon, the Huron Light Ship was anchored on a sandy shoal about six miles north of Port Huron for 50 years. When she was decommissioned in 1970, she was moved to Pine Grove Park, restored, and opened to the public as a museum.

800 Prospect Pl.
810-984-9760
porthuron.org/departments/parks_and_forestry

Tour: Blue Water Trolley

Explore the Port Huron area on this one-hour tour past dozens of city attractions, including the **Bridge to Bay Trail, the Fort Gratiot Lighthouse, Freighters Eatery & Taproom,** and a **Dairy Queen** ice cream shop. The Blue Water Trolley proudly charges riders just 10 cents to join the tour.

2021 Lapeer Ave.
810-987-7373
bwbus.com/blue-water-trolley

Trip Planning

Blue Water Area Visitors Bureau

500 Thomas Edison Pkwy., Suite 200
810-987-8687
bluewater.org

MUSKEGON
GRAND HAVEN
96
31
WYOMING
GRAND ISLAND
GRAND MARAIS
TAHQUAMENON FALLS STATE PARK
SAULT STE MARIE
MARQUETTE
MUNISING
SENEY
SENEY NWR
MANISTIQUE LAKE
HIAWATHA NATIONAL FOREST
DAFTER
ST JOSEPH ISLAND
TRENARY
ENGADINE
MANISTIQUE
DE TOUR VILLAGE
ST IGNACE
MACKINAC ISLAND
BOIS BLANC
NORWAY
ESCANABA
MACKINAW CITY
BEAVER ISLAND
CHEBOYGAN
BURT LAKE
MULLETT LAKE
BLACK LAKE
PETOSKEY
INDIAN RIVER
BOYNE FALLS
GAYLORD
GREEN BAY
WEST BRANCH
HOUGHTON LAKE
HARRISON
EVART
CLARE
WIXOM LAKE
MIDLAND
BIG RAPIDS
MT PLEASANT
SILVER LAKE SAND DUNES
SHELBY
WHITE CLOUD
ST LOUIS
HOWARD CITY
MICHIGAN
GRAND RAPIDS
ST JOHNS
PORTLAND
LAKE MICHIGAN
WYOMING
HOLLAND
LANSING
SAUGATUCK
HASTINGS
CHARLOTTE
ALLEGAN
SOUTH HAVEN
BATTLE CREEK
KALAMAZOO
41
77
28
2
35
68
32
33
75
61
10
127
66
46
52
21
69
37
131
94

GRAND HAVEN

WEST MICHIGAN HAS dozens of Lake Michigan beach towns. But few are as integrally connected to its shoreline as Grand Haven. The Grand Haven Channel borders downtown. Many restaurants, coffee shops, and boutiques lie just blocks away from golden beaches. And a popular boardwalk joins them all together in a walkable, bikeable pathway.

Although every season has its charm, Grand Haven comes to life in summer. Restaurants set up their umbrella tables. Campers vie for a coveted site on the sand. Young people cruise the downtown with open windows, and everyone wears flip-flops. Grand Haven can get busy. Find a spot to park and leave your car behind. It's easy to pedal or walk this small town.

There are at least nine public Lake Michigan beaches in Grand Haven. Grand Haven State Park features the city's iconic red lighthouse and great people watching. Rosy Mound has wooded hiking trails to a quiet beach, while Kirk Park offers a dog beach. Whether you want a wilderness experience or a lively pickup volleyball game with some new friends, Grand Haven has a beach for you.

Grand Haven State Park

1001 Harbor Ave. • 616-847-1309 • michigandnr.com/parksandtrails

This state park covers 48 acres of prime Lake Michigan lakefront and is the highlight of any visit to Grand Haven. The beach measures just a half mile in length but feels longer since it adjoins the Grand Haven City Park beach. It's an easy walk from the state park to the pier, with its distinctive catwalk and two cherry-red lighthouses. There's a large modern campground on the sand, an overnight lodge, a beach pavilion, and picnic tables. And Grand Haven's boardwalk leads from the park to downtown shopping and dining, easily reached on foot or bicycle.

Swimming and beachcombing are natural pastimes at Grand Haven State Park. But there's also good fishing here, which you can access by boat or off the end of the pier. Many of Grand Haven's annual summer festivals take place at least in part on the beach, including the Kite Festival, the Coast Guard Festival, and the Sand Sculpture Contest.

Grand Haven Lighthouses, Grand Haven State Park
(Courtesy of Visit Grand Haven)

Lighthouse Connector Park (Courtesy of Visit Grand Haven)

Lighthouse Connector Park

Harbor Dr. • 616-842-4499
grandhaven.org/visitors/parks/lighthouse-connector-park-the-boardwalk

Commonly called simply "The Boardwalk," Lighthouse Connector Park forms a one-and-a-half-mile link between the **Grand Haven Lighthouse** at the state park and **Chinook Pier Park**. The route follows the Grand Haven Channel all the way to Lake Michigan, providing scenic views of the waterway, the high dunes to the west, and the boats on the channel, both pleasure craft and Coast Guard vessels.

Besides offering a pleasant walking route, you'll find lots of attractions along Lighthouse Connector Park. Visit the farmers market, go mini golfing, or hit the playground at Chinook Pier. Stop for lunch, ice cream, or a cold beer as the Boardwalk approaches downtown. Learn about the Grand Haven–based Coast Guard Cutter *Escanaba*, which sank in World War II, at **Escanaba Memorial Park**. Then walk out to admire the brilliant red Grand Haven Lighthouses before sinking your toes in the sand at **Grand Haven State Park**.

Kirby House

2 Washington Ave. • 616-846-3299 • thegilmorecollection.com/kirbyhouse

Kirby House comes close to being one of those restaurants that truly offers something for everyone. This restaurant complex in downtown Grand Haven houses three dining rooms: **K2 Pizzeria**; the **Kirby House Grill**, a casual bar and grill; and the **Grill Room**, a fine-dining steak house.

The impressive Kirby House building began life as the Gildner Hotel in 1873. The large brick building dominates its corner of downtown, just steps away from the **Lighthouse Connector Path**, the **Grand Haven Channel**, and boutique shopping. There's a pleasant outdoor patio in summer.

K2 serves half a dozen prepared wood-fired pizzas, like the traditional Margherita. But a long list of toppings encourages visitors to create their own Neapolitan masterpieces. The Kirby House Grill serves a wide variety of options, from burgers and handhelds to Asian stir fries, wet burritos, and pastas. Downstairs, the upscale Grill Room offers a quieter, more formal atmosphere and a menu of steaks and seafood.

The Kirby House (Courtesy of the Kirby House)

Nearby Alternatives

Venue: Musical Fountain

Grand Haven's Musical Fountain has been entertaining visitors since 1962, when it was installed as the world's largest musical fountain. A fun choreography of colorful lights and dancing jets of water is set to music, ranging from John Phillip Sousa marches to Led Zeppelin hits, each evening after dark during the summer months.

Lynne Sherwood Waterfront Stadium, 1 N Harbor Dr.
616-935-3272
ghfountain.org

Outdoors: Lakeshore Bike Trail

Rolling dunes, a tunnel of trees, occasional glimpses of Lake Michigan, and half a dozen public parks await cyclists on the 20-mile Lakeshore Bike Trail. The paved route parallels Ottawa County's beautiful Lakeshore Drive and leads between two Lake Michigan state parks, **Grand Haven** and **Holland**.

14035 Lakeshore Dr.
616-842-4499
mitrails.org

Restaurant: Morningside Café

Grand Haven's hugely popular Morningside Café serves up hearty, scratch-made breakfast and lunch fare in a dining room of mosaics created from broken Fiestaware shards. Dig into fluffy omelets stuffed with chorizo and chiles, pancakes studded with Traverse City cherries and almonds, and a Southwestern-inspired array of scrambles, sandwiches, and salads.

711 Washington Ave.
616-844-1131
facebook.com/mstarcafe

Outdoors: Hemlock Crossing

Miles away from the beach, this park offers wooded trails, a nature center, a public observatory, and a kayak launch in the scenic Pigeon River valley. Hemlock Crossing is as popular in winter as in summer, when its trails open to some of the area's prettiest snowshoeing and cross-country skiing.

8115 West Olive Rd., West Olive
616-786-4847
miottawa.org/parks/hemlockcrossing.htm

Trip Planning

Grand Haven Area Visitors Center

225 Franklin Ave.
616-842-4499
visitgrandhaven.com

GRAND MARAIS
GRAND ISLAND
TAHQUAMENON FALLS STATE PARK
SAULT STE MARIE
MUNISING
SENEY
SENEY NWR
HIAWATHA NATIONAL FOREST
MANISTIQUE LAKE
DAFTER
ST JOSEPH ISLAND
TRENARY
ENGADINE
MANISTIQUE
DE TOUR VILLAGE
DRUMMOND ISLAND
ST IGNACE
MACKINAC ISLAND
BOIS BLANC
ESCANABA
MACKINAW CITY
CHEBOYGAN
MULLETT LAKE
BLACK LAKE
ROGERS CITY
HOWARD CITY
GRAND RAPIDS
WYOMING
HASTINGS
ALPENA
FLETCHER POND
ATLANTA
HUBBARD LAKE
HARRISVILLE
HURON NATIONAL FOREST
TAWAS CITY
STANDISH
SAGINAW BAY
WIXOM LAKE
CLARE
MIDLAND
SILVER LAKE SAND DUNES
SHELBY
WHITE CLOUD
MT PLEASANT
BAY CITY
ST LOUIS
SAGINAW
MICHIGAN
MUSKEGON
CLIO
GRAND HAVEN
ST JOHNS
OWOSSO
FLINT
LAKE MICHIGAN
PORTLAND
FENTON
LANSING
HOLLAND
SAUGATUCK
BRIGHTON
CHARLOTTE
ALLEGAN
ANN ARBOR
SOUTH HAVEN
BATTLE CREEK
KALAMAZOO
JACKSON

GRAND RAPIDS

MICHIGAN'S SECOND MOST populous city serves as the commercial and cultural hub of West Michigan. Set along the banks of the Grand River, within Michigan's fruit belt, and 25 miles from Lake Michigan, Grand Rapids attracts visitors with its parks, its locally sourced restaurant menus, family activities, and cultural offerings.

Grand Rapids' history is rooted in furniture, with more than 40 manufacturers located here in the early 1900s. The craftsmanship and wealth produced by that industry fostered a community still enamored of the arts. Grand Rapids is home to a professional symphony, a thriving theater community (professional and civic), Michigan's longest-running opera company, and its only professional ballet company. Grand Rapids so loves the arts that a beloved downtown sculpture, Alexander Calder's ***La Grande Vitesse***, is the city's logo.

In addition to the arts, you'll find in Grand Rapids a city of museums and organized sports, of green spaces and glass-and-steel office towers. You'll also discover a city that loves a cold glass of beer. More than 40 craft breweries lie within a 30-minute drive of Grand Rapids.

Frederik Meijer Gardens & Sculpture Park

1000 E Beltline Ave. NE
888-957-1580 • meijergardens.org

☑ In a city that loves its green spaces and fine art, Meijer Gardens combines the two. The 158-acre campus on Grand Rapids' northeast side is subdivided into smaller themed gardens, including Japanese, English perennial, woodland shade, farm, and children's gardens. A permanent collection of more than 300 sculptures lies spread across the property, some outdoors, some inside the conservatory.

Meijer Gardens' five-story glass conservatory features five climate and plant zones: tropical, arid, carnivorous, Victorian, and a seasonal display greenhouse. The conservatory houses rotating fine arts exhibits and hosts a number of the Meijer Gardens' most popular annual events, including Butterflies are Blooming and Christmas and Holiday Traditions, featuring dozens of trees decked out with holiday decor from around the world.

The **Frederik Meijer Gardens Amphitheater** hosts the park's annual Summer Concert Series, featuring performances from country to R&B, folk, rock, and pop groups for up to 1,900 people.

Meijer Gardens (Courtesy of Experience Grand Rapids)

Grand Rapids Art Museum (Courtesy of Experience Grand Rapids)

Grand Rapids Art Museum

101 Monroe Center St. NW • 616-831-1000 • artmuseumgr.org

✓ The first LEED Gold-certified art museum in the world opened in downtown Grand Rapids with the unveiling of the Grand Rapids Art Museum in 2004. But the museum traces its beginnings much further back to a community-wide public art association launched in 1901, reflecting the city's broad interest in the arts.

GRAM's permanent collection of 6,000 artworks ranges from Renaissance woodcuts to modern screenprints, from pen and ink to sculpture and textiles, from watercolor to mixed media, with an emphasis on 19th- and 20th-century European and American art. Highlights include works by Dürer, Rembrandt, Delacroix, Cassatt, Hassam, and Warhol.

While GRAM offers plenty in the way of fine art, the museum's artistic offerings include lectures, art camps, and hands-on artmaking clinics for childhood through adult. GRAM on the Green, free evenings of live local music, artmaking, and food trucks, takes place summers on the **Rosa Parks Circle**.

Founders Brewing Co.

235 Grandville Ave. SW • 616-776-2182 • foundersbrewing.com

☑ Founders Brewing opened its doors in 1997, the project of Mike Stevens and Dave Engbers in a time when craft brewing wasn't an everyday occurrence. From that uncertain beginning, Founders has grown to national recognition, operating out of taprooms in Grand Rapids and Detroit, employing over 600 employees, and selling their beers retail across all 50 states.

Visitors to Founders' Grand Rapids Taproom can choose from seasonal beers that range from session ales to porters, IPAs to stouts, including their famous Scotch ale, Dirty Bastard. The taproom's deli menu is heavy on sandwiches, stuffed thick with prime meats, cheeses, locally grown greens, and often topped by a Founders beer-infused barbecue sauce or mustard.

Founders is the most famous craft brewery in Grand Rapids, a city that relishes its beer-oriented reputation. But it's not alone. Among the metro area's 40 breweries, favorites include **Brewery Vivant, Grand Rapids Brewing, New Holland-The Knickerbocker**, and **Atwater**.

Founders Brewing Company (Courtesy of Experience Grand Rapids)

Nearby Alternatives

Museum: Gerald R. Ford Presidential Museum

The life, work, and legacy of America's 38th president are displayed in downtown Grand Rapids, where Ford grew up and served as a US Representative. Artifacts and interactive displays recount the president and first lady's lives and the Watergate scandal that led to Ford's appointment first as vice president, then as president of the US.

303 Pearl St. NW
616-254-0400
fordlibrarymuseum.gov

Outdoors: Millennium Park

This 1,400-acre jewel in Grand Rapids' wide assortment of parks ranks as one of the nation's largest urban green spaces. Millennium Park features six miles of Grand River frontage, boat rentals, a splash pad, swimming beach, picnic facilities, playgrounds, and paved trails for walking, cycling, and cross-country skiing.

1415 Maynard Ave. SW, Walker
616-791-2357
kentcountyparks.org/parks-trails/millennium-park

Venue: Van Andel Arena

Downtown Grand Rapids is home to a dozen music venues, performance halls, and theaters. The largest of them is Van Andel Arena, which seats up to 12,000. The arena is home to the **Grand Rapids Griffins**, but you can also catch headliner concerts by performers ranging from Kenny Chesney to Ariana Grande.

130 W Fulton St.
616-742-6600
vanandelarena.com

Museum: Grand Rapids Public Museum

The story of Grand Rapids is told through the exhibits of the Grand Rapids Public Museum. The historical museum touches on the city's Native American culture, early European settlement, and natural science with thousands of artifacts and interactive displays. Also popular at the museum are the 1928 **Spillman Carousel** and the **Roger B. Chaffee Planetarium.**

272 Pearl St. NW
616-929-1700
grpm.org

Trip Planning

Experience Grand Rapids

171 Monroe Ave. NW, Suite 545
616-258-7388
experiencegr.com

MICHIGAN
HOLLAND
WYOMING
SAUGATUCK
GRAND HAVEN
GRAND RAPIDS
MUSKEGON
LANSING
FLINT
SAGINAW
KALAMAZOO
BATTLE CREEK
BENTON HARBOR
ANN ARBOR
DEARBORN
SAGINAW BAY
MUNISING
SENEY
MANISTIQUE
HIAWATHA NATIONAL FOREST
MACKINAC ISLAND
ST IGNACE
MACKINAW CITY
CHEBOYGAN
ALPENA
TAWAS CITY
BAY CITY
MIDLAND
ALLEGAN
SOUTH HAVEN
HASTINGS
CHARLOTTE
PORTLAND
JACKSON
COLDWATER
HUDSON
ADRIAN
MONROE
NILES
THREE RIVERS

HOLLAND

FAMOUSLY FOUNDED BY Dutch settlers in the 19th century, Holland is known for tulips, wooden shoes, a historic windmill, and its annual spring flower festival, Tulip Time. All of those Dutch icons and more are present in this West Michigan community, but there's much more to the city than klompen dancers and tulips.

Holland is a city of private and public gardens, perhaps a holdover from all that tulip cultivation. It's a city bursting with blooms from early spring through fall. Its location on Lake Michigan translates into rich opportunities for outdoor recreation, from swimming and fishing on the beach to hiking, biking, and camping in the dunes. The city of Holland is also home to an abundance of parks, with playgrounds, picnic tables, and pickup basketball courts.

Theaters, the Holland Symphony, and art galleries offer plenty of cultural opportunities. Restaurants and breweries dot the downtown. And downtown shopping and dining are trouble-free no matter the season. Thanks to snowmelt, an underground hot water heating system, five miles of downtown sidewalks and streets are snow- and ice-free year-round.

Windmill Island Gardens

1 Lincoln Ave. • 616-355-1030 • cityofholland.com/471/Windmill-Island-Gardens

An authentic 90-foot Dutch windmill forms the centerpiece of Windmill Island. Built about 1760, **De Zwaan** (The Swan) was the last windmill exported out of the Netherlands when it was shipped overseas in 1964. De Zwaan was painstakingly reassembled piece-by-numbered-piece in downtown Holland, where visitors can walk through the windmill and see its workings grind grain just as it has since it was constructed more than 250 years ago.

Joining De Zwaan at Windmill Island are a dozen additional Dutch attractions, including a working street organ gifted by the city of Amsterdam after World War II, replica Dutch buildings like a fisherman's house and an inn, an antique carousel, and shops selling authentic Dutch Delft, cookies, cheese, and tulip bulbs.

The grounds at Windmill Island are planted with 150,000 tulips and other spring bulbs that burst into bloom in late April and early May. Once the tulips have expired, thousands of summertime perennials and annuals take their place.

Windmill Island Gardens (Courtesy of Amy S. Eckert)

Big Red, Holland State Park (Courtesy of Amy S. Eckert)

Holland State Park

2215 Ottawa Beach Rd. • 616-399-9390 • michigandnr.com/parksandtrails

There are few pastimes more relaxing than sinking your feet into the sugar sand beach on the Lake Michigan shore. Holland State Park offers about a half mile of sugar sand beach and is an immensely popular place to visit in summer for swimming, boating, and watching the sunset. The park offers terrific views of Holland's iconic **"Big Red"** lighthouse, which sits on the south side of the **Holland Channel** and is sadly seldom open to the public thanks to private property barriers.

In addition to the swimming beach, Holland State Park offers two large modern campgrounds. Book well in advance, as the campsites are popular. There's also an accessible playground, fishing and paddling opportunities, and connections to multiuse trails including the **Lakeshore Bike Trail**. A boardwalk follows the Holland Channel inland from the beach. A boat launch with a fish cleaning station is located one mile east of the park.

Boatwerks Waterfront Restaurant

216 Van Raalte Ave. • 616-396-0600
boatwerksrestaurant.com

✓ Over the course of its century-old life, the building that houses Boatwerks has served as an aggregate dock and storage facility, a coal dock, and a marine construction and dredging company. The building next door originally housed the Superior Ice Company, which harvested and stored ice from a frozen Lake Macatawa.

In 2006, these buildings on Lake Macatawa were converted into **Boatwerks Waterfront Restaurant** and **Boatworks Banquet and Catering**. Vintage photos and an antique Chris Craft boat within the restaurant building recall Holland's history as a boat manufacturing town. Large plate-glass windows take advantage of the restaurant's beautiful lake views, which only improve when Boatwerks' large outdoor patio opens in summer.

Boatwerks' menu offers a wide range of options. Lighter fare includes entrée-size salads and grain bowls, tacos, handhelds, and pizzas. Heartier entrées include Great Lakes walleye and perch, barbecue ribs, and hand-cut steaks.

Boatwerks (Courtesy of Amy S. Eckert)

Nearby Alternatives

Museum: Holland Museum

The story of Holland, from its Native American beginnings to its settlement by Dutch and Latin American immigrants, is told through artifacts and vintage photographs on the main floor of this grand colonnaded building. The museum's upper level houses the Dutch Galleries, with an impressive collection of 17th- to 20th-century artworks from the Netherlands.

31 W 10th St.
616-796-3329
hollandmuseum.org

Activity: Tunnel Park

A broad sugar sand beach is the highlight of this 22-acre park on Holland's northside. A unique concrete tunnel leads through a towering coastal dune for access to the water. On the inland side of the tunnel are a large playground, picnic facilities, and sand volleyball courts.

66 Lakeshore Dr. N.
616-786-4847
miottawa.org/parks/tunnel.htm

Discover: Veldheer Tulip Gardens

Holland's only tulip farm bursts into spectacular bloom each spring, when an estimated 5.5 million tulips blossom. Visitors can purchase tulip and other spring bulbs in the adjoining store, which also houses **De Klomp Wooden Shoe and Delft Factory**, with a Dutch-trained shoe carver and the only authentic Delft ceramics manufactory in North America.

12755 Quincy St.
616-399-1900
veldheer.com

Brewery and Restaurant: New Holland Brewing Co.

Holland's original craft brewery remains its largest, offering not only a dozen beers in its taproom at any given time, but a wide array of spirits as well. Dine on burgers, sandwiches, and gourmet pizzas in the two-story taproom or outdoors on New Holland's large outdoor patio.

66 E 8th St.
616-355-6422
newhollandbrew.com

Trip Planning

Holland Visitors Bureau

78 E 8th St.
616-394-0000
holland.org

PORTLAND
LANSING
CHARLOTTE
21
69
127
SAULT STE MARIE
MUNISING
SENEY
DAFTER
HIAWATHA NATIONAL FOREST
SENEY NWR
MANISTIQUE LAKE
ENGADINE
ST JOSEPH ISLAND
DE TOUR VILLAGE
DRUMMOND ISLAND
MANISTIQUE
ST IGNACE
MACKINAC ISLAND
BOIS BLANC
MACKINAW CITY
BEAVER ISLAND
CHEBOYGAN
BURT LAKE
MULLETT LAKE
BLACK LAKE
ROGERS CITY
INDIAN RIVER
PETOSKEY
ALPENA
THUNDER BAY
MANITOU ISLANDS
LUDINGTON
SILVER LAKE SAND DUNES
SHELBY
SEBEWAING
MARLETTE
MUSKEGON
CLIO
LAPEER
GRAND HAVEN
GRAND RAPIDS
ST JOHNS
OWOSSO
FLINT
FRANKENMUTH
OXFORD
WYOMING
FENTON
PONTIAC
HOLLAND
SAUGATUCK
HASTINGS
BRIGHTON
CHARLOTTE
DETROIT
ALLEGAN
ANN ARBOR
DEARBORN
SOUTH HAVEN
BATTLE CREEK
KALAMAZOO
JACKSON
BENTON HARBOR
JONESVILLE
ADRIAN
MONROE

LANSING

MICHIGAN'S STATE CAPITAL ranks as an obvious vacation destination for those who love history. A guided tour of Lansing's capitol building recounts the building's construction story as well as those of the characters who helped build it. Nearby, the Michigan Historical Museum adds depth to those stories, from its earliest residents to the mid-20th century.

Michigan's capital also offers a host of activities to entertain families. The **Impression 5 Science Center** ranks as one of the finest hands-on museums in the state, and **Potter Park** as one of its finest zoos. Spend a summer day at one of Lake Lansing's parks or bike the beautiful Lansing River Trail through Lansing and East Lansing.

East Lansing is home to Michigan State University, which offers a wealth of cultural attractions. The **Wharton Center for Performing Arts** features some of the world's top-rated artists in Broadway-style productions, musical concerts, and theatrical events. The striking **Eli and Edythe Broad Art Museum** exhibits contemporary art from around the world. And MSU draws sports fans to Spartan Stadium and the Breslin Center.

Michigan State Capitol

100 N Capitol Ave. • 517-373-2353 • capitol.michigan.gov

✓ When Michigan's capitol building was completed in 1879, it ranked as one of the few capitols in the nation to be topped with an impressive cast iron dome. Guided tours of the elegant Renaissance Revival building are enormously popular as they shed light on Michigan's history as well as on building details that might be overlooked on your own. (If you opt for a self-guided tour, a tour booklet will help you get the most out of your visit.)

Viewing the rotunda is a highlight on any tour of the capitol. Soaring over a floor constructed of 975 pieces of glass, the **capitol dome** soars 160 feet high and is covered with platinum and gold leaf stars to represent Michigan's limitless future. Other beautiful details include nine acres of hand-painted Victorian wall art, floor tiles bearing the remains of fossilized marine animals, and portraits of Michigan governors, US senators, and Michigan's only president, Gerald R. Ford.

Michigan State Capitol
(Courtesy of Michigan State Capitol Collection, photo by David Marvin)

Michigan Historical Museum (Courtesy of Michigan History Center)

Michigan Historical Museum

702 W Kalamazoo St. • 517-335-2573 • michigan.gov/mhc/museums/mhm

✔ There is no better place to learn the story of Michigan's evolution than the Michigan Historical Museum. The museum's exhibits spread across three stories, moving chronologically from the Anishinaabe people who occupied the state following the Ice Age through the middle of the 20th century.

An imposing white pine, Michigan's state tree, soars over the heart of the museum lobby, where the first floor hosts rotating exhibits on varied history themes, from women's suffrage in Michigan to the fight for civil rights. The museum's second floor features its permanent collection, beginning with Native American tools, dwellings, and interactive displays. Other exhibits include a look at Michigan's mining, lumbering, Great Lakes shipping, and Civil War history. The third floor wraps up with the more modern era, examining the state's place on the international stage in World War I and World War II, its manufacturing prowess, and the birth of the Motown sound.

The English Inn Restaurant and Pub

677 S Michigan Rd., Eaton Rapids
517-663-2500 • englishinn.com

The brick Tudor Revival English Inn was constructed in 1927 as Medovue, the elegant personal residence of Irving Reuter, general manager and president of Oldsmobile, and his wife Janet. Massive fireplaces, beautifully finished wood, and fine antiques filled the Reuters' 10,000-square-foot home while they lived and entertained here until 1934. The 15-acre grounds were crisscrossed by walking paths and planted in colorful flower gardens. In 1989, the property was restored and converted into a sophisticated B&B and fine dining restaurant.

Besides garnering attention for its beautiful building, the English Inn has won awards for the restaurant's lengthy fine wine list and its romantic ambience. Classic English Inn dishes include beef Wellington, lobster-stuffed walleye, and filet mignon, but the dinner menu also offers duck, seafood, and vegetarian options. The warm, wood-paneled Pub at the English Inn provides a more casual setting and menu. Choose from soups and salads, fish and chips, burgers, and sandwiches.

The English Inn (Courtesy of the English Inn)

Nearby Alternatives

Museum: Eli and Edythe Broad Art Museum

The striking angles of the glass and steel Broad Art Museum are especially eye-catching alongside the traditional brick and ivy-covered buildings of the MSU campus. The museum balances its sizable permanent collection of global contemporary art with works on loan to explore modern-day topics through a historical lens.

547 E Circle Dr., East Lansing
517-884-4800
broadmuseum.msu.edu

Venue: Wharton Center for Performing Arts

A mix of internationally famous blockbuster works and newly commissioned pieces by little-known artists fills the stage at the Wharton Center, the premier performing arts center on the MSU campus and in the Lansing area. Expect performances by internationally acclaimed ballet troupes and Broadway musicals as well as musical concerts and educational lectures.

750 E Shaw Ln., East Lansing
517-432-2000
whartoncenter.com

Educational Venue: Impression 5 Science Center

Taking its name from the five senses, Impression 5 brings scientific concepts within the grasp of young visitors through hands-on activities and games. The exhibit "Flow" is a two-story water-themed room, "Pop" explores the science of bubbles, and "Throwing Things" examines the aerodynamics of paper airplanes, baseballs, and air cannons.

200 Museum Dr.
517-485-8116
impression5.org

Outdoors: Lansing River Trail

More than 17 miles of paved multiuse trail parallels the Grand River, Red Cedar River, and Sycamore Creek. With boardwalk sections leading over water and wetlands, the trail guides cyclists and pedestrians through Lansing and East Lansing, through urban and rural areas, and into **Potter Park Zoo** and the MSU campus.

Grand and Red Cedar Rivers
517-483-4277
lansingtrails.org

Trip Planning

Greater Lansing Convention & Visitors Bureau

500 E Michigan Ave., Suite 180
517-487-0077
lansing.org

MUNISING
SENEY
SENEY NWR
MANISTIQUE LAKE
ENGADINE
MANISTIQUE
HIAWATHA NATIONAL FOREST
DAFTER
ST JOSEPH ISLAND
DE TOUR VILLAGE
DRUMMOND ISLAND
ST IGNACE
MACKINAC ISLAND
BOIS BLANC
MACKINAW CITY
BEAVER ISLAND
MANITOULIN
CHEBOYGAN
BURT LAKE
MULLETT LAKE
BLACK LAKE
ROGERS CITY
INDIAN RIVER
PETOSKEY
LAKE CHARLEVOIX
BOYNE FALLS
ALPENA
MANITOU ISLANDS
GAYLORD
FLETCHER POND
THUNDER BAY
TORCH LAKE
ATLANTA
HUBBARD LAKE
GLEN ARBOR
MANCELONA
HARRISVILLE
HOLLAND
SAUGATUCK
131
ALLEGAN
HARBOR BEACH
SEBEWAING
SANDUSKY
MARLETTE
LAPEER
FLINT
FRANKENMUTH
OXFORD
FENTON
PONTIAC
WYOMING
LANSING
HOLLAND
SAUGATUCK
HASTINGS
BRIGHTON
CHARLOTTE
DETROIT
ALLEGAN
ANN ARBOR
DEARBORN
SOUTH HAVEN
BATTLE CREEK
JACKSON
KALAMAZOO
BENTON HARBOR
JONESVILLE
THREE RIVERS
COLDWATER
ADRIAN
MONROE
HUDSON
NILES

SAUGATUCK

SAUGATUCK'S CREATIVE BENT stretches back over a century to 1910, when the Art Institute of Chicago established its **Ox-Bow School** here to offer instruction packaged with fresh air, natural beauty, inspiration, and respite as a counter to that offered at its urban campus. The move cemented Saugatuck as an art-centric destination in West Michigan.

Artists of all abilities continue to study at Ox-Bow's summer workshops. Other art-themed institutions like the **Art Barn**, the **Saugatuck Center for the Arts**, and two dozen acclaimed art galleries in town and in neighboring Douglas maintain Saugatuck's reputation as a creative, inspired, open-minded community, the Art Coast of Michigan.

Creativity in the arts spills over into Saugatuck's restaurant scene. The town's location in Michigan's fruit belt assures that once you've ordered your meal or handcrafted cocktail, it will arrive loaded with locally sourced ingredients. You'll also find locally brewed beer, Michigan-made wine and spirits, and lots of cozy inns and B&Bs. And when you're finished shopping for art and enjoying a fine dinner, the beaches that drew a century's worth of artists are just as beautiful as ever.

Saugatuck Dunes State Park

6575 138th Ave. • 269-637-2788 • michigandnr.com/parksandtrails

More than two and a half miles of sugar sand Lake Michigan beach lies protected within Saugatuck Dunes State Park. But you'll have to do some work to reach the water, and you'll be glad you did.

Thirteen miles of trails wind through the 1,000 acres of state park and the adjoining **Patty Birkholz Natural Area**. Over hardpacked soil made uneven with twisted tree roots, through sandy blowouts, over pine needle carpets and up forested backdunes, the trails allow visitors to immerse themselves in the beauty of Michigan's coastal forest before they emerge onto the Lake Michigan shore. Once there, they encounter a wild swath of beach: no restrooms, no picnic areas, and no shave ice stands, only miles of untouched Lake Michigan beach.

For the most direct hike to the beach, follow the yellow Beach Trail 0.75 miles one way. The red **Livingston Trail** measures 2.5 miles and is particularly popular with cross-country skiers.

Saugatuck Dunes State Park (Courtesy of Amy S. Eckert)

Saugatuck Chain Ferry (Courtesy of Felicia Fairchild)

Saugatuck Chain Ferry

Mary St. at the Kalamazoo River • 269-857-4261 • saugatuckcity.com/chain-ferry

☑ The Saugatuck Chain Ferry traces its roots to the Civil War era. The ferry, *Diane*, travels across the Kalamazoo River by a chain that links to anchors on either side of the water. Ferry operators hand crank the boat from one side to the other during summer months, a trip that departs roughly every 15 minutes depending upon demand. The *Diane* is the only remaining hand-cranked chain ferry remaining in the US, and her operation is always weather dependent.

Boarding the Saugatuck Chain Ferry allows visitors in downtown Saugatuck easy access to attractions on the west side of the Kalamazoo River. Once there, it's a pleasant walk to **Mt. Baldhead Park** with its 303-step wooden staircase to the top of the Mt. Baldhead dune. Continue down the Lake Michigan side of **Mt. Baldy** to reach **Oval Beach**, voted on multiple occasions as one of the finest beaches in the nation.

Bowdie's Chophouse

230 Culver St. • 269-455-5481 • bowdieschophouse.com

✓ Bowdie's sits within a former residence in downtown Saugatuck. Its cozy, intimate space is dimly lit, the interior done up with distressed wood and leather worn to the point of buttery softness. This chophouse fills with locals, who dress in jeans and sweatshirts and laugh easily. But the restaurant also exudes an elegant, Rat Pack–era vibe, with crisp black and white table linens, crystal wine glasses, and a menu that includes some of the finest steaks you will ever bite into.

A lengthy vintage, handcrafted cocktail menu often marks the start of an evening at Bowdie's. The wine list, while only moderately long, offers a wonderfully eclectic selection of Old and New World wines by the glass or the bottle. While flavorful, melt-in-your-mouth steaks form the centerpiece of the menu, other entrées include seasonally prepared chicken and salmon as well as shareables like escargots, lobster mac, and potatoes au gratin. There's a full-service bar and indoor and outdoor seating.

Bowdie's Chophouse (Courtesy of Amy S. Eckert)

Nearby Alternatives

Venue: Saugatuck Center for the Arts

Theater, concerts, art exhibits, film, art education, and workshops. The Saugatuck Center for the Arts combines a host of art displays and instruction under a single roof. Programming is available for all ages, from watercolor painting to forest bathing and creative dining. Check out the center's film festivals.

400 Culver St.
269-857-2399
sc4a.org

Outdoors: Oval Beach

Celebrated as one of the nation's best beaches, Saugatuck's Oval Beach sits along a broad swath of golden sand and against a backdrop of rolling dunes. There's easy parking on the beach but during the busy summer months, taking the chain ferry and making the half-mile walk may be a more enjoyable and practical option.

Perryman St. and Oval Beach Dr.
269-857-1986
saugatuckcity.com/oval-beach

Venue: Armstrong De Graaf International Fine Art

Michigan's oldest continuously operating art gallery makes its home in Michigan's Art Coast. Tracing its history back to 1946, the Armstrong De Graaf gallery displays and sells contemporary and historic artworks, including sculpture, acrylic paintings, art glass, and mixed media works from its location in downtown Saugatuck.

403 Water St.
269-857-2230
jpettergalleries.com/Armstrong-degraaf

Trip Planning

Saugatuck/Douglas Area Convention & Visitors Bureau

95 Blue Star Hwy.
269-857-1701
saugatuck.com

SAULT STE MARIE
DAFTER
MUNISING
SENEY
SENEY NWR
MANISTIQUE LAKE
HIAWATHA NATIONAL FOREST
HIAWATHA NATIONAL FOREST
ST JOSEPH ISLAND
ENGADINE
DE TOUR VILLAGE
DRUMMOND ISLAND
MANISTIQUE
ST IGNACE
MACKINAC ISLAND
BOIS BLANC
MACKINAW CITY
BEAVER ISLAND
CHEBOYGAN
BURT LAKE
MULLETT LAKE
BLACK LAKE
ROGERS CITY
PETOSKEY
INDIAN RIVER
ALPENA
FLETCHER POND
THUNDER BAY
ATLANTA
HUBBARD LAKE
HARRISVILLE
TAWAS CITY
ALLEGAN
SOUTH HAVEN
KALAMAZOO
94
SAGINAW BAY
SEBEWAING
BAY CITY
SAGINAW
MARLETTE
MICHIGAN
MUSKEGON
CLIO
LAPEER
GRAND HAVEN
GRAND RAPIDS
ST JOHNS
OWOSSO
FLINT
FRANKENMUTH
OXFORD
LAKE MICHIGAN
WYOMING
PORTLAND
FENTON
HOLLAND
LANSING
SAUGATUCK
HASTINGS
BRIGHTON
CHARLOTTE
ALLEGAN
DETR
ANN ARBOR
DEARBORN
SOUTH HAVEN
BATTLE CREEK
KALAMAZOO
JACKSON
BENTON HARBOR
JONESVILLE
THREE RIVERS
COLDWATER
ADRIAN
MONROE
HUDSON
NILES

SOUTH HAVEN

SOUTH HAVEN'S BLACK River and its seawalls divide the city's Lake Michigan beachfront in half. **North Beach** lies an easy walk to South Haven's terrific **Michigan Maritime Museum** and to numerous historic B&B inns. The attractions recall South Haven's historic role as a premier grower and supplier of fruit to Chicago. Even as ships delivered boxes of peaches and apples to the Windy City, Chicago's urban dwellers made their way across Lake Michigan to escape into cozy inns and the fresh, cool air of South Haven.

South Beach lies nearest South Haven's downtown. Walking from the city to the beach is a pleasant pastime, the walkway bordered with overflowing flower beds and picture-postcard views. The walk follows the South Pier to the iconic red South Haven Lighthouse, which is perhaps even more spectacular in winter, when encased in icicles like a turreted castle.

Besides beaches—and there are seven public beaches and Lake Michigan access points in total in South Haven—the city is known for its blueberries. South Haven's favorite fruit is feted each August at the National Blueberry Festival and finds its way onto menus throughout the city.

South Beach

60 Water St. • southhavenmi.gov/parks_and_recreation/beaches.php

✓ Located on the southern side of the Black River that divides South Haven's Lake Michigan beachfront in two, South Beach is the sole public beach on the south side of the channel. South Beach also lies closest to the city's downtown shopping and dining. It's an easy and pleasant walk to the beach from downtown, a gentle downward slope leading the way to the water. As you walk, you'll stroll along a path that's lined with colorful, overflowing flower beds, the golden beachfront and the brilliant red **South Haven Lighthouse** and its catwalk in view. Park benches along the way allow you to settle in and enjoy the scene.

Swimming, beachcombing, fishing, and building sandcastles are the most popular pastimes at South Beach, with walking the South Pier out to the South Haven Light right up there. A transfer station near the playground on South Beach makes this Lake Michigan strand one of the most accessible in West Michigan.

South Haven Lighthouse, South Beach
(Courtesy of Dylan Nelson, South Haven Van Buren County CVB)

Museum Maritime Museum (Courtesy of South Haven Van Buren County CVB)

Michigan Maritime Museum

260 Dyckman Ave. • 269-637-8078
michiganmaritimemuseum.org

✓ Exhibits at the Michigan Maritime Museum focus on Great Lakes commercial and leisure travel past and present. The exhibits are spread across five museum structures and help visitors immerse themselves in the sailing life, from the 18th century to the present.

The maritime museum's fleet of vessels allows a sailing experience rarely found at a museum. Available vessels include a replica 19th-century sloop, a replica 19th-century electric river launch, a 1941 USCG motor lifeboat, a 1929 Chris Craft Cadet, and a 1921 racing yacht, all of which offer brief cruises.

In addition to maritime exhibits, a series of Great Lakes lectures and festivals brings greater depth to a museum visit, with topics ranging from iconic lighthouses to shipwrecks. An annual antique and classic boat show is popular, as is the **Maritime District Boardwalk**, which begins at the museum and includes historic markers to help pedestrians visualize the busy harbor as it once was.

Clementine's

500 Phoenix St. • 269-637-4755
ohmydarling.com

It's difficult to miss Clementine's. The restaurant sits within a magnificent South Haven landmark, the former Citizen's State Bank building, constructed in 1896. The stately red brick building resembles something of a castle, with its soaring turret, and has been home to Clementine's since 1982. The restaurant still utilizes two of the bank's original vaults as storage. Its imposing wooden bar immediately stands out, and its interior is packed with antiques and a nice array of South Haven historical photos and memorabilia.

The menu at Clementine's offers a bit of something for everyone. Soups, burgers and sandwiches, pasta, steaks, barbecue ribs, and a nice selection of fish. The salads on Clementine's menu are especially creative, including house greens topped with local strawberries, walnuts, and chicken breast or a romaine salad with cavatappi pasta, parmesan, tomatoes, and Caesar dressing. Clementine's is locally famous for their homemade onion rings.

Clementine's (Courtesy of South Haven Van Buren County CVB)

Nearby Alternatives

Discover: DeGrandchamp Farms

This South Haven mainstay includes 200 acres of blueberries in an area famous for the fruit. Pick your own blueberries to take home with you, shop for fresh-picked, dried, and frozen berries, or pick up one of a dozen other blueberry goodies, from jams and barbecue sauces to blueberry plants for your home garden.

76241 14th Ave.
269-637-3915
degrandchamps.com

Discover: Crane Orchards

South Haven may be famous for its blueberries, but this region of Michigan grows plenty of other fruits. Head to Crane Orchards for U-Pick peaches, sweet cherries, and 20 different varieties of apples. In the fall, buy pumpkins, hop aboard a hayride, and lose yourself (temporarily) in Crane's 20-acre corn maze.

6054 124th Ave., Fennville
269-561-8651
craneorchards.com

Activity: *Friends Good Will*

A replica of the 1810 topsail merchant sloop of the same name, the *Friends Good Will* offers cruises of Lake Michigan daily in the summer. Visitors are put to work assisting with the hoisting and lowering of sails and steering. Historical sails, sunset sails, pirate sails, and Great Lakes maritime educational sails are all available.

260 Dyckman Ave.
269-637-8078
michiganmaritimemuseum.org

Outdoors: Kal-Haven Trail

This much-loved rail trail leads bicyclists and pedestrians from South Haven to Kalamazoo on a hard-packed surface that's appropriate for all abilities. The route passes through small towns, beneath a canopy of hardwood trees, and past historic sites marked by interpretive signs. The trail measures 34 miles end-to-end.

51 Bailey Ave.
269-685-6851
kalhaven.org

Trip Planning

South Haven Visitors Bureau

546 Phoenix St.
800-764-2836
southhaven.org

LAKE MICHIGAN
131
ALLEGAN
SOUTH HAVEN
KALAMAZOO
94
60
THREE
MUNISING
SENEY
SENEY NWR
MANISTIQUE LAKE
ENGADINE
HIAWATHA NATIONAL FOREST
TRENARY
MANISTIQUE
ESCANABA
DAFTER
ST JOSEPH ISLAND
DE TOUR VILLAGE
DRUMMOND ISLAND
ST IGNACE
MACKINAC ISLAND
BOIS BLANC
MACKINAW CITY
BEAVER ISLAND
CHEBOYGAN
BURT LAKE
MULLETT LAKE
BLACK LAKE
ROGERS CITY
INDIAN RIVER
PETOSKEY
LAKE CHARLEVOIX
BOYNE FALLS
GAYLORD
FLETCHER POND
ATLANTA
MANITOU ISLANDS
HUBBARD LAKE
WYOMING
HOLLAND
SAUGATUCK
HASTINGS
LANSING
CHARLOTTE
ALLEGAN
SOUTH HAVEN
KALAMAZOO
BATTLE CREEK
ANN ARBOR
JACKSON
BENTON HARBOR
JONESVILLE
THREE RIVERS
COLDWATER
ADRIAN
HUDSON
OWOSSO
CLIO
FENTON
PORTLAND

KALAMAZOO

ART AND CREATIVITY abound in Kalamazoo. Credit the city's large population of young, forward-thinking residents for its inventiveness and vitality. Kalamazoo is home to three colleges: Western Michigan University, Kalamazoo College, and Kalamazoo Valley Community College. The city is also home to a world-class art museum, the **Kalamazoo Institute of Arts**; a premier concert and performing arts venue, **Miller Auditorium**; and a host of live theater and music stages.

If Kalamazoo is a city steeped in artistic creativity, it is also a city surrounded by natural beauty. Six hiking and biking trails draw people out into the rolling hills and forests of the surrounding countryside, the most popular being the **Kal-Haven Trail** to South Haven, the **Kalamazoo River Valley Trail**, and the **Maple Hill Mountain Bike Trail**. Kalamazoo is also a city of parks, including downtown's Bronson Park, and the surrounding agricultural area means you'll find it easy to dine on locally sourced menus.

If you enjoy shopping, head to downtown Kalamazoo and the Kalamazoo Mall. The nation's first outdoor pedestrian shopping mall opened here in 1959.

Kalamazoo Institute of Arts

314 S Park St. • 269-349-7775 • kiarts.org

The Kalamazoo Institute of Arts has been making art accessible to its community since 1924. Ten galleries display fine artworks from around the globe, some from its permanent collection of 5,000 pieces, others from traveling exhibitions.

Of its sizable permanent collection, the Kalamazoo Institute of Arts offers a special emphasis on its works of 20th-century American painting and sculpture. Highlights include works by Childe Hassam, Charles M. Russell, Robert Mapplethorpe, Marc Chagall, and Andy Warhol. The museum also offers a fine collection of African American works, alongside European prints, photography, and contemporary works of ceramics.

The KIA offers free Sunday drop-in tours. Visitors can go into greater depth as they walk through the galleries with trained docents who share the background behind a number of important artworks. The **KIA Gallery Shop** is considered particularly good and will allow you to bring a souvenir of ceramic, paper, or fabric art home with you.

Kalamazoo Institute of Arts (Courtesy of Discover Kalamazoo)

Air Zoo (Courtesy of Discover Kalamazoo)

Air Zoo

6151 Portage Rd. • 269-382-6555
airzoo.org

What began as a personal collection of vintage World War II aircraft morphed into the Kalamazoo Aviation History Museum in 1979. Now known as the Air Zoo, a reference to the animal names of the aircraft in the original collection—a Wildcat, Hellcat, Bearcat, and a Flying Tiger—this attraction surprises most visitors. Yes, aviation and military history buffs enjoy the 100+ air and space artifacts that now make up the Air Zoo's collection. But the sheer volume and variety of planes and the indoor flight-themed amusement park rides make the Air Zoo a universal crowd-pleaser. The quality of the museum's collection and restorations has status as a **Smithsonian Affiliate**.

The Air Zoo's collection explores flight history from the 1700s through the jet and space ages. A few of the artifacts on display include a Montgolfier balloon, a World War I–era Sopwith Camel, and the World War II–era Wildcats, Hellcats, and Bearcats that launched the Air Zoo 40 years ago.

Bell's Eccentric Café

355 E Kalamazoo Ave. • 269-382-2332 • bellsbeer.com/eccentric-cafe

✓ Larry Bell entered the beer business as a home-brewer in the 1980s, making beer for friends and selling home-brewing equipment from a shop in downtown Kalamazoo. His success in creating Bell's Brewery is legend, the brewery now a mainstay in West Michigan and its iconic beers, Third Coast, Oberon, and Two Hearted among them, recognized across the country.

Bell's Eccentric Café allows beer lovers to choose from 20 different drafts paired with a menu that's just a bit eccentric. Nibble on snacks and lighter fare, such as the house favorite brown butter and garlic popcorn, or a helping of poutine, Great Lakes whitefish dip, or house-made pimento cheese. If you're hungry for something more substantial, order from a lineup of creative burgers—perhaps a chipotle cherry jam and goat cheeseburger, or a cudighi sausage patty—a falafel sandwich, or tacos filled with Amber Ale and chili braised pork. In warm weather, enjoy the beer garden and patio.

Bell's Eccentric Café (Courtesy of Bell's Brewery)

Nearby Alternatives

Museum: Gilmore Car Museum

The personal vintage car collection that belonged to Donald Gilmore in the 1960s has exploded to become one of the nation's largest and most complete automobile museums. More than 500 vehicles are displayed on the property, beginning with an 1899 Locomobile Steam Car and extending through the muscle car era.

6865 Hickory Rd., Hickory Corners
269-671-5089
gilmorecarmuseum.org

Museum: Kalamazoo Valley Museum

A three-story shadow-box wall of historic Kalamazoo artifacts greets visitors to this downtown museum, which has been free since its founding in 1881. Galleries focus on history, science, and technology. Hands-on exhibits explore human health, Great Lakes geography, climate, and forensics, among other topics. A Children's Landscape room includes preschool-age activities.

230 N Rose St.
800-772-3370
kalamazoomuseum.org

Venue: Miller Auditorium

Located on the Western Michigan University campus, Miller Auditorium ranks as one of the finest and largest performing arts venues in West Michigan. The auditorium frequently hosts the **Kalamazoo Symphony Orchestra** and stages live theater performances, musical concerts, Broadway-style shows, comedy events, and public lectures.

1341 Theatre Dr.
269-387-2300
millerauditorium.com

Outdoors: Kalamazoo River Valley Trail

This paved, multiuse trail spans 24 miles of Kalamazoo County, passing through quiet wooded parks, through downtown Kalamazoo, and along the Kalamazoo River along the way. The western terminus joins the **Kal-Haven Trail** if you want to extend your ride, and a northern spur leads to the **Kalamazoo Nature Center**.

10th Street near H Avenue
269-342-1740
kalcounty.com/parks/krvt

Trip Planning

Discover Kalamazoo

240 W Michigan Ave.
269-488-9000
discoverkalamazoo.com

SENEY
SENEY NWR
MANISTIQUE LAKE
HIAWATHA NATIONAL FOREST
DAFTER
ST JOSEPH ISLAND
ENGADINE
NISTIQUE
DE TOUR VILLAGE
DRUMMOND ISLAND
ST IGNACE
MACKINAC ISLAND
BOIS BLANC
MACKINAW CITY
BEAVER ISLAND
MANITOULIN ISLANDS
CHEBOYGAN
BURT LAKE
MULLETT LAKE
BLACK LAKE
ROGERS CITY
INDIAN RIVER
PETOSKEY
ALPENA
LAKE HURON
GLEN ARBOR
FRANKFORT
BEAR LAKE
MANISTEE
BALDWIN
MANISTEE NATIONAL FOREST
SHELBY
WHITE CLOUD
HOWARD CITY
OXFORD
PONTIAC
BRIGHTON
DETROIT
DEARBORN
94
ST C
CAN
HARBOR BEACH
SANDUSKY
MARLETTE
MUSKEGON
CLIO
LAPEER
PORT HURON
GRAND HAVEN
GRAND RAPIDS
ST JOHNS
OWOSSO
FLINT
FRANKENMUTH
OXFORD
PORTLAND
WYOMING
FENTON
HOLLAND
LANSING
PONTIAC
SAUGATUCK
HASTINGS
BRIGHTON
CHARLOTTE
ALLEGAN
DETROIT
LAKE ST CLAIR
ANN ARBOR
DEARBORN
SOUTH HAVEN
BATTLE CREEK
KALAMAZOO
JACKSON
CANADA
BENTON HARBOR
JONESVILLE
THREE RIVERS
COLDWATER
ADRIAN
MONROE
HUDSON
NILES

DETROIT

MICHIGAN'S LARGEST CITY has garnered attention for the recent renewal of its downtown. After a period of decline, Detroit rebounded with dozens of new boutique hotels, independent restaurants, and cocktail bars, many of them in beautifully restored Art Deco buildings.

Cultural institutions like the **Detroit Institute of Arts**, the **Motown Museum**, the **Detroit Symphony Orchestra**, and the **Detroit Historical Museum** rank among the state's finest, and they tell the story of Michigan's history, culture, and innovation like no place else. Organized sporting events have always been popular in "The D." Head to **Comerica Park** (where the Tigers play), **Ford Field** (where the Lions play), or **Little Caesars Arena** (home to the Pistons and the Red Wings) and join thousands of Detroiters whose can-do spirit translates into fiercely loyal fandom.

Many first-timers to Detroit are surprised at the city's outdoor recreation. **Belle Isle** is a popular urban retreat and has been for generations. Detroit River Sports guides kayaking tours of the Detroit River, recounting its unique ecology and history. And the **Detroit Riverwalk** wraps history, culture, and nature into a single package.

Detroit Institute of Arts

5200 Woodward Ave. • 313-833-7900 • dia.org

✓ The DIA was founded in 1885 and has consistently ranked among the top 10 art museums in the US, with more than 65,000 pieces on display, from ancient cultural touchstones to modern-day masterpieces. The museum was built and supported by Detroiters convinced of the value of fine art and went on to become one of the city's most famous and beloved institutions.

Highlights of the museum's permanent collection include *Self Portrait*, the first Van Gogh to enter an American museum; Bruegel's *The Wedding Dance*; and *Officer of the Hussars* by Kehinde Wiley, acclaimed contemporary African American portraitist. The DIA's most famous works may be the *Detroit Industry* murals painted by Diego Rivera in the 1930s. The paintings, which are widely accepted as America's finest Mexican murals, cover all four walls of the museum's **Rivera Court**. Head to the DIA's gift shop for Detroit-centric gifts, including books, jewelry, and ceramics.

Detroit Industry, Detroit Institute of Arts (Courtesy of Amy S. Eckert)

Motown Museum (Courtesy of Motown Museum)

Motown Museum

2648 W Grand Blvd. • 313-875-2264 • motownmuseum.org

✓ The musical icons of a generation found early success at this humble house with the big *Hitsville USA* sign emblazoned across the front. The house and eventually three additional neighboring residences formed the headquarters of Berry Gordy's Motown music label beginning in 1959. Following the techniques of Detroit's automotive industry, Gordy brought hundreds of talented, unpolished young performers through the doors at Motown, taught them harmony, poise, and stagecraft, then sent them out to change the landscape of American music forever.

Exhibits at the Motown Museum display album art, music and video clips, memorabilia, and costumes worn by Motown's biggest stars. Visitors also get the opportunity to walk through the studio where its finest performers recorded their music: Smokey Robinson, Stevie Wonder, Diana Ross, Gladys Knight, Marvin Gaye, the Temptations, and Michael Jackson. And a nice gift shop sells Motown memorabilia and recordings.

San Morello

1400 Woodward Ave. • sanmorello.com

✓ Shinola, the craft watchmaker, turned heads in 2018 when the Detroit-based company opened its first hotel. Set in the heart of a revitalized Detroit, the luxury boutique hotel took over five conjoined, century-old buildings, restored aging facades and disheveled stairwells, and crafted new guest rooms, gathering spaces, and a restaurant emphasizing Detroit-made art, fabrics, and furnishings.

Shinola's signature fine dining restaurant is San Morello. Located on the hotel's ground floor, on the corner of Woodward Avenue and Grand River Avenue, the restaurant is inspired by the design and flavors of Southern Italy and Sicily. An interior of caramel-colored wood and ceramic tiles in royal blue, burgundy, and amber tones give an immediate feeling of warmth. The menu features wood-fired pizzas and flatbreads, and house-made gnocchi and pasta, dressed with flavorful sauces of mushrooms, gorgonzola, and roasted tomatoes. And the wood-fired grill is kept hot to roast fresh fish, chicken, and ribeye steaks.

San Morello (Courtesy of Nicole Franzen)

Nearby Alternatives

Outdoors: Detroit Riverwalk The sparkling Detroit Riverfront forms a beautiful backdrop for walking, running, or cycling in downtown Detroit. The five-mile paved Riverwalk parallels the Detroit River and includes numerous attractions: a lighthouse, wetlands, a carousel of Detroit River animals, public art, **Aretha Franklin Amphitheater**, numerous parks, and the landmark towers of the **Renaissance Center**, GM's world headquarters.

Atwater St. at Renaissance Dr. W
detroitriverfront.org

Restaurant: The Apparatus Room The award-winning Apparatus Room sits within the **Detroit Foundation Hotel** in Detroit's former fire department headquarters. Structural elements from 1929 include oversized fire doors and fire poles. The menu features pasta with a Detroit Coney Dog–inspired sauce and inventive preparations of classic seafood, steak, and pot roast. Enjoy a cocktail at the bar, lit with dozens of Edison bulbs.

250 W Larned St.
detroitfoundationhotel.com/apparatus-room

Outdoors: Outdoor Adventure Center Michigan's great outdoors comes to downtown Detroit at the OAC. Designed to whet city dwellers' appetite for Michigan's state parks, the OAC's interactive games and activities allow visitors to ride simulated snowmobiles and ORVs, paddle a kayak, climb a tree, feel the splash of a waterfall, and learn archery.

1801 Atwater St.
844-622-6367
michigan.gov/oac

Outdoors: Belle Isle State Park The Detroit River's Belle Isle has long been a favorite among residents, with its varied outdoor activities in the heart of downtown Detroit. Now a state park, the island offers kayaking, SUP, bicycle and foot trails, a lighthouse, a swimming beach, and an aquarium. The freshly renovated **Anna Scripps Whitcomb Conservatory** will reopen in 2024.

99 Pleasure Dr. • 313-821-9844
michigan.org/property/belle-isle-park

Trip Planning

Detroit Metro Convention & Visitors Bureau

211 W Fort St., Suite 1000
800-338-7648
visitdetroit.com

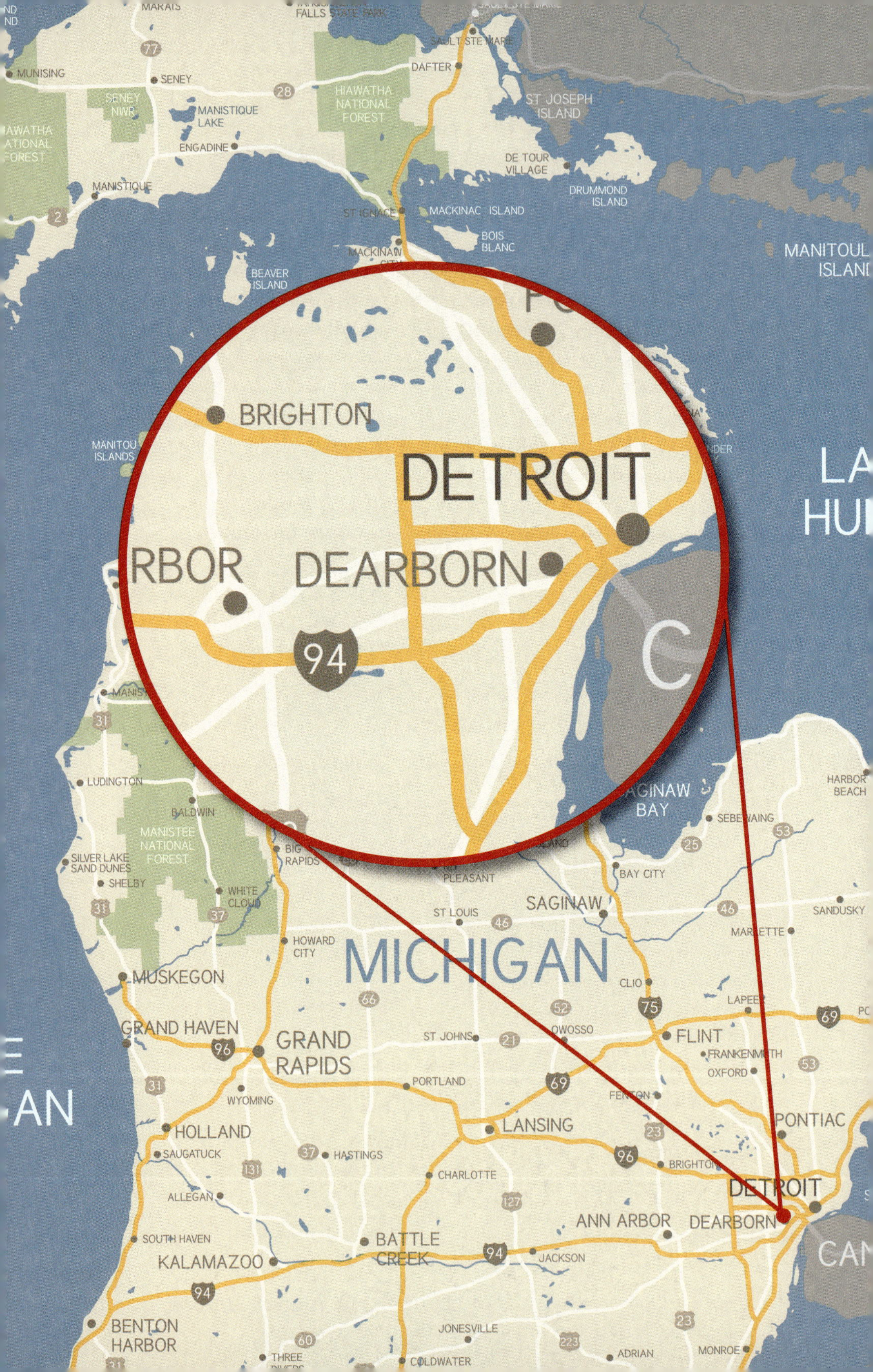
BRIGHTON
DETROIT
DEARBORN
RBOR
94
MICHIGAN
MUNISING
SENEY
MANISTIQUE LAKE
ENGADINE
MANISTIQUE
SENEY NWR
HIAWATHA NATIONAL FOREST
SAULT STE MARIE
DAFTER
ST JOSEPH ISLAND
DE TOUR VILLAGE
DRUMMOND ISLAND
ST IGNACE
MACKINAC ISLAND
BOIS BLANC
MACKINAW CITY
BEAVER ISLAND
MANITOULIN ISLAND
MANITOU ISLANDS
LUDINGTON
BALDWIN
MANISTEE NATIONAL FOREST
SILVER LAKE SAND DUNES
SHELBY
WHITE CLOUD
BIG RAPIDS
MT PLEASANT
SAGINAW BAY
SEBEWAING
HARBOR BEACH
BAY CITY
SAGINAW
ST LOUIS
SANDUSKY
MARLETTE
HOWARD CITY
MUSKEGON
CLIO
LAPEER
GRAND HAVEN
GRAND RAPIDS
ST JOHNS
OWOSSO
FLINT
FRANKENMUTH
OXFORD
PORTLAND
WYOMING
FENTON
PONTIAC
HOLLAND
LANSING
SAUGATUCK
HASTINGS
BRIGHTON
CHARLOTTE
DETROIT
ALLEGAN
ANN ARBOR
DEARBORN
SOUTH HAVEN
BATTLE CREEK
KALAMAZOO
JACKSON
BENTON HARBOR
JONESVILLE
ADRIAN
MONROE
COLDWATER
THREE RIVERS

DEARBORN

FRENCH SETTLERS ESTABLISHED the city of Dearborn in the 18th century, dividing the fertile land along the Rouge River into ribbon farms. A century later, Henry Ford was born on a Dearborn farm. It's probably no accident that the automotive pioneer eventually constructed Ford Motor Company's headquarters and his personal estate in the city of Dearborn.

The traces of Henry Ford are obvious in modern-day Dearborn. The **Henry Ford Museum of American Innovation** and **Greenfield Village**, which combine to represent some of the finest historical collections outside Washington, DC, both trace their roots to Ford's personal collections of household items, tools, vehicles, even historic buildings and businesses. Henry Ford's estate, **Fairlane**, is in the midst of a lengthy restoration, but the grounds are open to visitors.

Wayne County is home to more people of Middle Eastern descent than anyplace outside the Middle East. Dearborn is home to many of those immigrants, from Lebanon, Palestine, Iraq, and Yemen. As a result, visitors enjoy some of the finest Mediterranean food on the continent, from family-owned bakeries and takeaway spots to fine dining restaurants.

The Henry Ford Museum of American Innovation

20900 Oakwood Blvd. • 313-982-6001 • thehenryford.org

✓ Henry Ford loved collecting "relics," as he called them, items that represented a piece of Americana, that encapsulated a time gone by, and that symbolized industrial progress. A personal collection that began with books and timepieces went on to include a wide assortment of antiques, including machinery, tools, and household items. By the 1920s, Henry Ford had amassed the world's largest collection of Americana, and it was all located on his property in Dearborn.

Today, Ford's collections—and more besides—are on display at the Henry Ford Museum. Unsurprisingly, the museum displays a wide array of vehicles, including Henry Ford's 1901 Model T, the Montgomery city bus in which Rosa Parks refused to give up her seat, the Wienermobile, and five presidential limos, including the car in which Kennedy was assassinated. Other notable items in the collection include George Washington's army cot, Lincoln's stovepipe hat, and the chair in which he was sitting when he was assassinated.

The Henry Ford Museum of American Innovation (Courtesy of Visit Detroit)

Greenfield Village (Courtesy of Visit Detroit)

Greenfield Village

20900 Oakwood Blvd. • 313-982-6001
thehenryford.org/visit/greenfield-village

☑ Henry Ford's love of collecting Americana extended from the objects of everyday life to the buildings in which those lives played out. Begun first as Ford's attempt to preserve places important to him and his wife Clara, like Ford's boyhood home and the Bagley Avenue shed where he built his first car, Greenfield Village encompasses 80 acres of historic buildings. Visitors can walk through **Thomas Edison's Menlo Park** and F**ort Meyers laboratories; the Wright Brothers' Dayton, Ohio, bicycle shop**; and the **homes of poet Robert Frost and dictionary compiler Noah Webster**. They can also tour colonial houses from New England, a 19th-century Maryland plantation and its slave quarters, even a Cotswold cottage from England and a Swiss chalet.

A fun way to tour sprawling Greenfield Village is via an authentic **Model T ride**. Because the property is outdoors and structures are not generally heated, Greenfield Village is open only during warm-weather months.

Al Ameer

12710 W Warren Ave., Dearborn • 313-582-8185
27346 Ford Rd., Dearborn Heights •
313-565-9600 • alameerrestaurant.com

In a city known for its Middle Eastern food, Al Ameer stands out. The restaurant opened in Dearborn in 1989, focused on authentic Mediterranean cooking using only fresh local ingredients and from-scratch preparations. In 2016 partners Kahlil Ammar and Zaki Hashem were rewarded when the **James Beard Foundation** presented Al Ameer with the American Classics Award, given to businesses that "have timeless appeal and are cherished for quality food that reflects the character of their community."

Al Ameer's two Dearborn-area restaurants serve Lebanese favorites, beginning with fresh raw fruit and vegetable juices and smoothies. Dishes of creamy-smooth hummus and baskets of steaming pita are prepared fresh every morning. Savory, vertically grilled meats are thinly sliced for shawarmas. It doesn't take long before diners' orders of shish kebabs, lamb chops, ghallaba, chicken cream chops, and sides of fattoush, tabbouli, baba ghanoush, and labneh fill the table.

Al Ameer (Courtesy of Edsel Little)

Nearby Alternatives

Tour: Ford Rouge Factory Tour

After a multisensory film celebrating the history and innovation behind the Ford brand, visitors tour the Rouge Factory, which was founded in 1903 by Henry Ford himself. The immense assembly plant has produced Model As, tractors, military vehicles, and muscle cars, and today manufactures the standard F-150 pickup and the all-electric F-150 Lightning.

20900 Oakwood Blvd.
313-982-6001
thehenryford.org/visit/ford-rouge-factory-tour

Museum: Arab American National Museum

The nation's only Arab American Museum tells of the community's history and contributions dating back to 16th-century North America through vintage photos and passports, hand-knotted prayer rugs, and interactive displays. The second floor shines a spotlight on famous Arab Americans in the fields of entertainment, science, sports, and politics.

13624 Michigan Ave.
313-429-2535
arabamericanmuseum.org

Discover: The Detroit Zoo

More than 2,000 animals reside on the Detroit Zoo's 125 acres. In addition to beloved animal favorites, like giraffes, zebras, kangaroos, and gorillas, the zoo includes the world's largest penguinarium with 75 birds as well as one of North America's largest polar bear habitats, the Arctic Ring of Life.

8450 W 10 Mile Rd., Royal Oak
248-541-5717
detroitzoo.org

Restaurants and Bars: Corktown

Detroit's oldest surviving neighborhood reflects the flavor and energy of a revitalized Detroit. Choose from one of a dozen vibrant independently owned restaurants and bars, including **Slows Bar BQ, Bobcat Bonnie's, Mercury Burger & Bar, Ima Izakaya, The Sugar House, Johnny Noodle King, Lucky Detroit**, and **Two James Spirits**, among many others.

Michigan Ave. between the Fisher and Lodge Fwys.

Trip Planning

Detroit Metro Convention & Visitors Bureau

211 W Fort St., Suite 1000
800-338-7648
visitdetroit.com

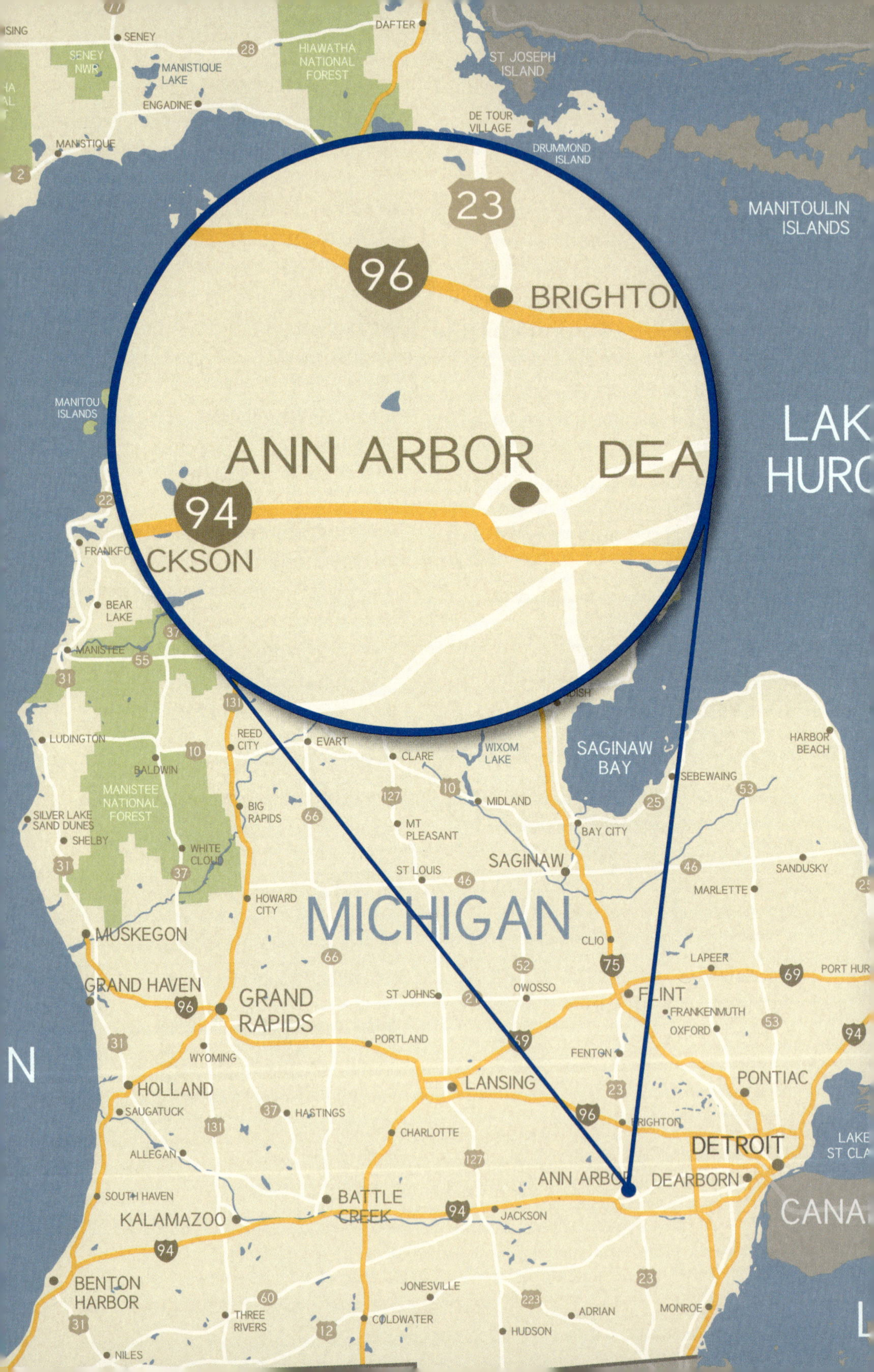
ANN ARBOR
BRIGHTON
DEA
CKSON
MICHIGAN
LAKE HURON
SAGINAW BAY
MANITOULIN ISLANDS
ST JOSEPH ISLAND
DRUMMOND ISLAND
DE TOUR VILLAGE
DAFTER
SENEY
SENEY NWR
MANISTIQUE LAKE
HIAWATHA NATIONAL FOREST
ENGADINE
MANISTIQUE
MANITOU ISLANDS
FRANKFORT
BEAR LAKE
MANISTEE
LUDINGTON
BALDWIN
MANISTEE NATIONAL FOREST
SILVER LAKE SAND DUNES
SHELBY
WHITE CLOUD
REED CITY
EVART
CLARE
WIXOM LAKE
MIDLAND
BIG RAPIDS
MT PLEASANT
BAY CITY
SEBEWAING
HARBOR BEACH
SAGINAW
ST LOUIS
SANDUSKY
MARLETTE
HOWARD CITY
MUSKEGON
CLIO
LAPEER
PORT HURON
GRAND HAVEN
GRAND RAPIDS
ST JOHNS
OWOSSO
FLINT
FRANKENMUTH
OXFORD
PORTLAND
WYOMING
FENTON
PONTIAC
HOLLAND
LANSING
SAUGATUCK
HASTINGS
CHARLOTTE
ALLEGAN
DETROIT
LAKE ST CLAIR
ANN ARBOR
DEARBORN
SOUTH HAVEN
BATTLE CREEK
KALAMAZOO
JACKSON
CANADA
BENTON HARBOR
JONESVILLE
THREE RIVERS
COLDWATER
HUDSON
ADRIAN
MONROE
NILES

ANN ARBOR

THE UNIVERSITY OF MICHIGAN permeates life in Ann Arbor, lying near the center of the city and fully integrated with its commercial and social life. On home football game days, Wolverine fans fill the downtown, their maize-and-blue shirts brightening the sidewalks and the city's restaurants until kickoff lures them away to the game at "The Big House."

The presence of the U of M also benefits Ann Arbor culturally. Institutions like the **University of Michigan Museum of Art**, the **Museum of Natural History**, the **Power Center for the Performing Arts**, and numerous fine art galleries offer immense benefits to the city's residents and visitors no matter where their university allegiances lie.

Ann Arbor is a town that loves good food, and you'll find plenty to choose from on any visit. Ranked among the best food towns in the Midwest by *Midwest Living* magazine, Ann Arbor relies on inventive preparations of locally sourced food. **Zingerman's Community of Businesses** leads the way, with a deli, bakehouse, candy manufactory, creamery, sit-down restaurant, and more.

University of Michigan Museum of Art

525 S State St. • 734-764-0395
umma.umich.edu

☑ One of the nation's first and finest university art museums, the UMMA has been collecting artworks and sharing them with the public since 1856. Art is so vital to the U of M's calling that the subject appears in the university's mission statement, asserting that art is a "human essential and a foundation that helps to define our future."

The UMMA's 21,000 artworks are located within its original home, the colonnaded Alumni Memorial Hall of 1946, and within the addition of the Maxine and Stuart Frankel and Frankel Family Wing of 2009. There's a strong emphasis on European art from the Renaissance to the 19th century, Chinese and Japanese art from antiquity to the 19th century, African art of the 19th and 20th centuries, and American art from the 19th century to the present. Highlights include masterpieces by Whistler and Picasso, Chinese and Japanese paintings and ceramics, and sculpture from central Africa.

University of Michigan Museum of Art (Courtesy of Destination Ann Arbor)

Ann Arbor Hands-On Museum (Courtesy of Destination Ann Arbor)

Ann Arbor Hands-On Museum

220 E Ann St. • 734-995-5439
discoverscienceandnature.org

✔ This downtown Ann Arbor museum divides its interactive play stations into 10 different sensory-themed rooms centered largely on STEM topics. Included hands-on activities revolve around building simple machines, understanding human health, water science and play, light and optics, and a simulated country store. A preschool gallery provides the museum's youngest visitors with water tables, ball runs, and building stations with a variety of construction blocks. A nice museum store offers lots of educational toys and games for sale.

Affiliated with the Ann Arbor Hands-On Museum is the **Leslie Science and Nature Center** northeast of downtown. In addition to all the attributes you would expect from a public park—hiking trails, bird- and wildlife-watching opportunities, and natural scenery—the center includes a nature playscape, a raptor enclosure, and a Critter House with regional natives like frogs, turtles, snakes, and salamanders. Ongoing projects include a waterplay area and a treescape climbing structure.

Zingerman's Delicatessen

422 Detroit St. • 734-663-DELI (3354) • zingermansdeli.com

✓ What began in 1982 as a neighborhood deli committed to quality ingredients and employee empowerment has become an Ann Arbor institution. **Zingerman's Community of Businesses** incorporates a dozen food-oriented organizations including a coffee roastery, a creamery making cheese and ice cream, a bakehouse, a candy maker, two sit-down restaurants, and a deli. There's also a training company that helps other food businesses improve service and management.

But Zingerman's Delicatessen was where it all began, and the sandwich shop remains one of the most popular places in Ann Arbor to grab a meal. Made-to-order sandwiches are stuffed with Black Angus corned beef and pastrami and free-range chicken, chicken salad, and turkey. Veggies are fresh as can be and grown nearby. The deli store includes a grocery, where you can buy those ingredients as well as quality oils, mustards, bread, and deli staples like pickles and potato salad. Zingerman's adjacent **Next Door Café** sells coffee drinks, cakes, and pies.

Zingerman's Delicatessen (Courtesy of Destination Ann Arbor)

Nearby Alternatives

Discover: University of Michigan Museum of Natural History

The Museum of Natural History evokes wonder and curiosity in a three-story building that includes the world's only male and female mastodon skeletons assembled side by side. A host of exhibits cover the subjects of evolution, microbiology, geology, Michigan's flora and fauna, and a life-size reconstruction of a Quetzalcoatlus pterosaur in the atrium.

1105 N University Ave.
734-764-0478
lsa.umich.edu/ummnh

Tour: Motawi Tileworks

Handcrafted ceramic art tiles are produced in this facility west of Ann Arbor. Inspired by the Arts and Crafts, Art Nouveau, and midcentury modern movements and by designers like Frank Lloyd Wright and Yoshiko Yamamoto, the showroom sells tiles individually as art pieces or in quantity for larger installations. Tours are available.

170 Enterprise Dr.
734-213-0017
motawi.com

Venue: Michigan Stadium

Affectionately known as "The Big House," Michigan Stadium ranks as the nation's largest athletic arena and is one of the most iconic stadiums in the US. Whether visits coincide with a game or not, visitors may tour the field, the press box, the locker room, and the premium seats.

1201 S Main St.
facilityrentals.ath.umich.edu

Venue: Michigan Theater

The Michigan Theater dates from 1928 and still uses its original stage, pipe organ, and orchestra pit. Celluloid and digital films are on the bill, often introduced by an organ concert, as are performances by the **Ann Arbor Symphony Orchestra, the University Musical Society**, and the **Not Just for Kids** children's live theater series.

603 E Liberty St.
734-668-8397
michtheater.org

Trip Planning

Destination Ann Arbor

315 W Huron St., Suite 340
734-995-7281
annarbor.org

Wine Grapes
(Courtesy of Amy S. Eckert)

Index

Eli and Edythe Broad Art Museum, East Lansing (Courtesy of Amy S. Eckert)